The Power of Joy

The Ultimate Guide to Living Your Best Life Ever

KELLEY CUNNINGHAM

 FriesenPress

One Printers Way
Altona, MB R0G 0B0
Canada

www.friesenpress.com

Copyright © 2022 by Kelley Cunningham
First Edition — 2022

Illustrator: Barbara Rosini

ISBN
978-1-03-912610-7 (Hardcover)
978-1-03-912609-1 (Paperback)
978-1-03-912611-4 (eBook)

Self-Help, Motivational & Inspirational

Distributed to the trade by The Ingram Book Company

To my dearest Jeffery,

You've always inspired so much joy within my spirit—your unwavering love and amazing encouragement, perpetually ignites a eternal flame of freedom, courage and a cunning confidence to soar optimistically towards each new dream and endeavor I explore—always feeling a giddy-delight of infinite possibility—YOU Rock my world!!!

Our twenty-eight year and counting miraculous love story started as a remarkable love at first sight encounter—a synergy of love and joy that began on a fateful night under a midsummer's moon lite sky—TRULY A MAGICAL MOMENT CAPTURED IN TIME!!!

We've stayed dedicated to designing a life filled with the same love and joy, one that defies all circumstance. Our faith and never surrender attitude has driven our dreams to infinite heights—much higher than either of us could have ever dreamt or thought possible. Proving that impossible isn't apart of our path.

Even now as a writer, written words can not truly convey how extremely lucky and loved I feel by your presents in my life—you are a gift from God. And as I have always insisted, our love is a match made in heaven for only God could have so seamlessly orchestrated our initial encounter.

Love you always,
Kelley Xo 24

To my three beautiful, beautiful, beautiful blessings,
Savannah, Sienna & Liam,

Also a love at first sight encounter and unconditional love, making
me a mama! Each of you inspire joy—the light of love in my life.

My greatest blessings,
My BIGGEST successes,
Being your mama is the purest proudest part of my life,
Each of you bring so much love to my life.

I pray for and wish each of you best life ever status and a beyond
beautiful joyful live—dream BIG be the BIGGEST dreamer and
ALWAY REMEMBER THAT YOU ARE THE MAGIC IN THE
MOMENT!!! All of you have GREATNESS within you and possess
infinite potential for GREATNESS out into the world. I will always
be your BIGGEST FAN AND CHEERLEADER!!!

Love you, Mom Xo

Acknowledgments

Dear Erin Aideen Fuller,

My dearest friend, you've been my greatest cheerleader, confidant and coach. You've not let me sacrifice a minute of JOY—questioning or second guessing my passions and path to writing my book of joy.

I feel beyond grateful & very blessed to have such an incredible friend who supported me every step of the way!!

"Stay Gold" my lovey, sweet friend. Xo

Dear Barbara Rosini,

You are magical, I absolutely appreciate your dedication to this book.
Your illustrations have magically transformed my words into immaculate images. You've perfectly captured the essence of my ideas & analogies within your amazing drawings. Giving the reader an opportunity to delve even deeper into the energy and spirit of joy!
I will admire & most humbly hold your works of art in my heart forever. I am also most grateful to gain a new friendship.

Thank you, Kelley

In loving memory of my Dad Walter Roland Stewart "Rolly".
I will be forever grateful for your unconditional love.

Table of Contents

Acknowledgments v

Preface ix

Introduction xi

Chapter One Lasting Happiness Is Joy 1

Chapter Two The Ripple Effect of Joy 15

Chapter Three Warrior Spirit 27

Chapter Four Autonomy 39

Chapter Five A Warrior in Faith 49

Chapter Six Peacefulness 61

Chapter Seven Meditation and Mantras 79

Chapter Eight Hello, It's Your Intuition Calling 91

Chapter Nine Run Your Own Race 99

Chapter Ten Patience with Persistence 113

Chapter Eleven Faith Over Fear 125

Chapter Twelve Present Moment Mindset 137

Chapter Thirteen Lead with Love 153

Chapter Fourteen Passions Are Popping 163

Chapter Fifteen Value Your Values 181

Chapter Sixteen Dust Settles. I Don't 189

Chapter Seventeen An Attitude of Gratitude 199

Chapter Eighteen Harmony 213

Chapter Nineteen Harmonious Balance 221

Conclusion 231

ABOUT THE AUTHOR 235

Preface

Each of us has a unique story to tell. It's my belief that, when we boldly share our strengths and struggles, we gain an important opportunity to inspire others, while at the same time launching ourselves further on our own life travels. In the last few years, my journey has become quite literally intwined with the power of joy.

I could never have imagined the extreme losses and challenges that would become trials in my life, which we will explore in this book. I can say with certainty, though, that faith, love, and joy set a bold courage in motion inside me, even when I faced overwhelming uncertainty.

To be clear, though you'll find that I do periodically reference faith, and even God, this is not a book about religion or religious beliefs. Faith means different things for different people. Whether you have faith in yourself, the universe, or even just in the inevitability of death and taxes, faith impacts us all. My personal faith includes God, but while he played a part in my personal journey, his presence is not required in yours. While he inspired the journey I set out on, in terms of this book, it is the journey itself that matters.

When my journey began, a deliberate energy of joy surfaced within my spirit, flowing swiftly into my heart when I needed it most. When I started exploring how to tap into the magical, lifting power of joy, it became a key tool to strengthen my inner spirit after my incredible husband, Jeffery, who is an amazing dad to my three awesome kids and the love of my life, suffered a traumatic brain injury (TBI) in a "non-contact" men's hockey league.

This and a series of other overwhelming life circumstances tried their hardest to suffocate my faith with fear, and steal my joy through sorrow. But I fought back! Fiercely. I replaced feelings of helplessness with faithfulness, and reframed feelings of lack with those of love in order to protect my precious family. I was determined not to let our circumstances take complete control over our lives. And, if I am brutally honest, I had never fought so flipping hard for anything in my life. I fought like a warrior through each day, empowered by my faith, moments of joy, and the belief that my family deserved the grace to get through this turbulent season without feeling robbed of those moments of time.

It was in the process of his healing that I discovered an inner passion to inspire joy in others as well. I gained a greater understanding of how to support others when I became certified as a professional life coach and started my own business, becoming the C.J.O. (Chief Joy Officer) of JoyINC. I am passionately driven to encourage the lasting power of joy in everyone I meet, and that is what this book is all about.

In its pages, I'll be sharing tidbits from my own story to explain why I am so diligently campaigning for the advantages that joy offers us all. When encouraging joy, I am speaking from my heart and drawing on my own personal life experience. This ultimate guide establishes and reflects on my truest intent: to lift your spirit and life with the powerful energy of joy. Joy has made my life much more meaningful, and I want you to have a more intimate relationship with joy as well. By the end of this book, I hope you feel empowered to move forward towards your best life ever—a life filled with joy!

Kelley D. Cunningham
C.J.O, BA
January 23, 2021
Oakville, Ontario, Canada.

Introduction

"If you carry joy in your heart, you can heal at any moment."
– Carlos Santana

My life journey has led me to explore and examine the strength of joy. I've found that joy is a magical source of internal energy—a miraculous energy—which delivers a powerful strength to continually refuel your spirit, allowing it to soar. Joy can lift your spirit to surpass any obstacle daring enough to cross your path. Joy lets you aspire above and beyond life's adversities to claim a *"best life ever"* status. Joy has undeniably lifted and enlightened my life, and I truly believe the power of joy can lift your spirits and allow them to soar as well.

My goal is to evoke a peaceful revolution of joy within your spirit, so that you will soar to immeasurable heights in life. This *can* happen, simply by embodying the power of joy. When you do this, the spirit of joy will lift you to new heights of happiness, while making the world a brighter place for us all. And *that* is exactly what sparked me to write this book. In these pages, you'll find straightforward encouragement to inspire you to tap into the amazing phenomenon of joy.

Joy most definitely has the ability to provide you with a constant stream of strength. It's a powerful tool for your mind, body, and soul. Joy magnifies our inner vision, enlightening us on our journey towards recognizing our own intrinsic ability to actively live our best life.

Everyone Deserves Their *Best Life Ever*

Everyone deserves the opportunity to claim *"best life ever"* status. This guide encourages you to embrace each day as a gift, even when life throws you unexpected curveballs. The practical tips and tools throughout this guide will map out the power of joy through inspirational and essential encouragement, lifting you to catch joy even during the most turbulent times. The power of joy softens the impact of unfair setbacks in life, while cheering you on to achieve your *best life ever*. I truly believe that you deserve to be living your best life, and I will whole-heartedly back-up my unquestionable truth by encouraging you with the infinite power of joy.

Whether you're consciously aware of it or not, you possess the ability to channel internal surges of joy outwards, strengthening your everyday life. A surge of joy releases inner strength, giving rise to the resilient stance of a warrior spirit. We'll talk later about what it means to have a warrior spirit, but know that this is an inner strength and resiliency that can light even the dimmest of spirits through life's darkest of days. And it is accessible to you through joy.

Joy flows from our spirit via numerous pathways, such as happiness, faith, gratitude, harmony, peace, and love. These pathways harness the power of joy, channeling it outwards from our spirit. I consider the above-mentioned six pathways to be key tools in unlocking the renewing energy of joy. These six primary vessels stream joy throughout all of life's adventures. The power of joy will encourage you to actively engage in living life with an exuberant intent to thrive.

When these pathways are consciously applied to your life, they become powerful tools to activate our senses with joy, while eagerly providing a heightened awareness for you to tap into the strength of joy and lift your spirits, regardless of the circumstances.

The Discoveries Awaiting You

In each chapter, you'll find fun, relatable analogies to outline the concepts we discuss, which will bring us closer to experiencing a lasting connection with joy. You'll find personal experiences, stories, and ideas—validated with fact-based scientific findings—throughout this guide.

Along the way, you'll discover a framework of ideas to support the bond of joy with happiness, faith, gratitude, harmony, peace, and love. I articulate how each of these pathways directly connects with the feeling of joy. Each concept shares a unique relationship, which directly releases the energy of joy, thus perpetuating the internal power of joy within your own spirit.

By consistently engaging in a joyous state of mind, you create a glorious and abundant resource to help with living your best life ever. Everyone has the opportunity to extract the strength of joy simply by being aware of what brings you the most joy and applying that, along with some key tools, to your everyday life. In this book, I will give you simple tips and tools, so you can tap into your internal treasure trove of joy at any time and in any place. When you actively commit to seeking joy, it becomes easy to adopt these simple ideas in your own life.

With every skill and talent, you must focus, work hard, and make a commitment to it before you can obtain increased levels of success. Joy is a learned skill and is no different. Some people will connect with joy more easily than others, but practicing positivity, kindness, self-love, and believing you deserve a joyful life will open your heart and mind to accept the power of joy in your life.

Living each day with an open mind, and being consciously aware of what brings you the most joy, will create a deeper journey with joy. You'll then further develop joy simply by spending more time immersed in joyful activities or in mindful moments. The more awareness you create around what brings you joy, the easier it will become to welcome joy into your life. When your mind and heart are open to receiving joy, joy will become a continual source of strength. However, you need to be *open* to receiving joy into your life for its power to truly thrive. Joy generates a stronghold of resilience within your heart, pulling you back on track when life tries its best to drag you sideways. I have experienced the stronghold power of joy many times in my life.

Each journey in life has a starting point. Let's begin our journey to awakening a *peaceful revolution of joy* in your life. Consider me your friendly neighborhood messenger of joy—an energetic, lovable, joy-seeker, cheering you on through your own discovery process of exploring what joy means to you. Imagine this as a guided tour, similar to the ones on those exciting, exotic travel-destination shows, or perhaps as you've experienced first-hand on a guided-adventure tour. Let's treat this as a magical, mystical, miraculous, joy-seeking exploration where the destination starts and ends within your own heart.

My Journey of Joy

In a fabulously fantastic leap of faith, my husband, Jeffery, our three beautiful children, and I took a courageous and calculated risk for our young family in November 2011, when we moved from Toronto, Canada, to Northwest Arkansas, USA. With an enormous adventure ahead of us, I beamed with a blissful feeling of joy and gratitude in my heart. I felt joy for the opportunity, for the adventures that awaited us, and for our loving family unit. Our oldest daughter, Savannah, was five; Sienna, our second daughter, was four; and Liam, our son, turned two years old the day before we all boarded the plane to Arkansas. Our new home proved to be a beautiful place to raise a family.

At that point in our lives, Jeffery and I had been married over ten years and been together for more than sixteen years. We are soulmates, destined by God's grace and goodness to meet under a moonlit summer's sky many years ago in a heartwarming moment that could've been taken straight from a dreamy romance novel.

Jeffery and I have always shared the magnificent and magical strength of faith. Together, we believe that anything and everything is possible, when you're equipped with faith, optimism, and determination. With faith (no matter what that looks like for each individual), we can obtain everything we set our sights on. *Our* faith is powered by a positivity that has fueled the strength of joy, allowing it to surge through our lives.

Even in troublesome times, we have continued forward with faith, and that faith has given us grace in each season. It's been our rock. It's propelled us triumphantly through life. And our move—over more than a thousand miles, between two countries, and with three tiny people in tow—was no exception. We believed we would succeed and thrive, and I say (as humbly as possible) that we did. In Northwest Arkansas, the Cunningham family thrived in all areas of our lives, well beyond even our most abundant predictions. God is good, and we activated his goodness simply by believing.

Northwest Arkansas (NWA) is also known as "Walmart country," as it's home to the biggest retailer in the world and is the original site of the very first Walton's five-and-dime store, which was the predecessor to what we all know now as Walmart. It's a beautiful, lush area where everyone and everything thrives on the success of Walmart Inc. Many top destination reviewers list it as one of the best places to live and raise a family in North America, and I agree.

There's a charming, quintessentially all-American, small-town feel, dynamically combined with the creature comforts of a metropolitan city. There's an incredible children's museum, and it's home to Crystal Bridges, an amazing American art gallery. NWA is a perfect place to raise a family, and I could not deny that, when we were there, we were living our best lives ever!

Our family life thrived. We had great friendships, a beautiful lifestyle, and numerous work successes. It was the very essence of a balanced, abundant family life. Neighbors were extremely friendly and welcoming, which created a rich sense of community. Everyone seemed to share values and a genuine sort of kindness that illuminated the neighborhood. Jeffery and I would laugh and joke, saying that our neighborhood was as if Pleasantville met Edward Scissorhands, and we delighted in it! We embraced the neighborhood, feeling blessed to experience such wonderful surroundings, and taking a lot of pride in our calculated risk to relocate our young family.

We were very grateful for our five blissful years there before venturing back to Canada to be closer to family in the fall of 2016. As we reluctantly said goodbye to our utopia-style life, we tried to embrace our new journey with the same faith, determination, and optimism that we'd embraced the previous one, five years earlier.

I know, right? If Arkansas was such a perfect fit, why did we move away from that beautifully blessed life? I sometimes indulge in wondering about that myself. It was the allure of sunny California that led us back to Canada. *Wait! What?* Nope, you didn't miss anything! As discombobulated as it sounds, our family's unrequited love for southern California were what set us in motion to leave Arkansas.

Jeffery works for SpinMaster, one of the world's leading toy and children's entertainment companies, and our family was extremely excited when he negotiated a relocation to southern California! In July of 2015, we were making plans to enjoy fun in the sun for the rest of our lives when we returned to Canada for our annual summer visit. That was when our focus shifted 180 degrees.

We learned that my fun-loving father-in-law, Bill, who was five years cancer-free from both colon and rectal cancer, had now been diagnosed with a second primary site of cancer. This time, it was his kidneys. We were also stunned by the news that Jeffery's younger brother, Luke, was headed into what would be a long, nasty, drawn-out divorce.

We were forced to confront the fact that my parents were seniors now, and my dad had several chronic health concerns. All of these discoveries played a key role in our decision to return to our roots to support our family. Thankfully, Jeffery persuaded his bosses to realign with the changes, so in a matter of moments, we were headed in completely the opposite direction.

So, now we were California dreaming in a Canadian destination. We tried our best to capture a southern California feel along the shorelines of Lake Ontario, Canada, and on many levels, we did just that. We were determined to have it all—the best of both worlds! We were daring enough to dream, and those daring dreams became our reality. We stayed determined, and our dreams came true.

Leading with a love for California, and lending our love to our family, seemed to create the harmonious balance we were striving for, so we could thrive in this unexpected season of life. We enjoyed the west coast lifestyle we'd been dreaming of while also supporting our family on Canadian soil. In lieu of a Pacific Ocean view, we discovered our dream home, nestled in the heart of Olde Oakville, a quaint area in the city of Oakville, on the shores of Lake Ontario, only minutes outside of Toronto. Little did we know the tidal wave of events that would hit us next, testing my every ability to hold joy in my heart.

Chapter One
Lasting Happiness Is Joy

*Happiness is smiling when the sun's out. Joy is
dancing in the downpour.*
– Unknown

Many people use joy and happiness interchangeably without ever
giving it much thought. My personal experiences, particularly from
after our family moved back to Canada—which I'll share with you
shortly—have led me to interpret joy and happiness as two distinct
entities with a unique partnership. The union between joy and happiness plays a key role in creating a longer lasting, sustainable energy
of joy.

Imagine for a moment that you had, in your hand, a source for
abundant happiness. It's happiness with *staying power*—happiness
that comes as a constant stream in your life. How would this influence your everyday life? Is achieving a constant state of happiness
even possible? Let's explore.

A constant state of happiness within our heart is called joy. When
transient happiness becomes permanent, it becomes joy. When we
are consciously aware of what makes us happy, we can build on
nurturing that happiness, one moment at a time. Happiness doesn't
have to be fleeting. It can actually work as a continuous strength

1

resting in our heart. When we recognize that, it opens multiple possibilities and pathways for joy. And thus, happiness that rests in your heart creates a more lasting attitude of joy.

Joy *is* an attitude. It's a state of mind and always stays within your heart, ready to uplift your spirits, therefore creating the possibility for a constant state of happiness in your life. Inner joy can be tapped into at any given moment. It's a powerful strength, especially in challenging circumstances—a strength that's always accessible to those who believe in the power of joy.

Happiness is the foundation for experiencing a joy-filled life. Happy experiences give everyone the power, in that moment, to receive joy. So, when we build on happiness by connecting happy moments, memories, and ideas in our thoughts, we in turn develop the staying power of joy.

The staying power of joy happens when we realize that happy moments can be manifested at any time. Joy is based on your personal belief, not on a single happy experience. We all have the ability to tap into an endless abundance of joy.

Some people are more in tune with the strength of joy, and they can apply joy more freely in their lives, boosting their spirit every day. But joy is in *all* of us. We must diligently drive forward with a genuine intent to be happy in order to truly feel we're living a happy life. When we let every happy-life encounter unify within our thoughts, we manifest the lasting energy of joy. But this is easier said than done when life places challenges in our path.

A Sudden, Sideswiping Challenge

Just weeks after we returned to Canada, my husband, Jeffery, was quite literally swept sideways. While playing in a non-contact, men's hockey game, an opponent swept Jeffery off his feet by hooking his hockey stick in front of Jeffery's legs at shin level. The aggressive slice of the stick swept Jeffery's feet into the air, and he came crashing down directly onto his face.

Jeffery woke up a few moments later in a pool of his own blood. He had been wearing a helmet, but the damage still included a broken nose, bruising, cuts, and scrapes. The impact caused his lower jaw to temporarily slip over his top jaw, leaving his upper gums almost black in color. Worst of all, he smacked down on the left side of his forehead and injured the frontal lobe of his brain.

The brain is composed of many parts, one of which is the frontal lobe. As the name suggests, the frontal lobe is at the front of the skull, near the forehead. The frontal lobe actually consists of a pair of lobes, commonly termed as the right and left frontal cortex. They control important cognitive skills such as emotional expression, problem solving, memory, language, and judgment. It is, in essence, the "control panel" of our personality and our ability to communicate. This part of the brain works in concert with other regions to control the overall functions of the brain. For instance, memory formation is not a product of one brain region but multiple brain regions working together.

The brain tends to rewire itself to recover from an injury, but this does not in any way mean that all patients will fully recover from a frontal-lobe injury, or that they will do so quickly. As we discovered in the long weeks, months, and years following the accident, Jeffery's injury was serious. The massive cognitive impact left him unable to work and coping with chronic pain.

We are grateful and feel extremely blessed that Jeffery was eventually lucky enough to heal from his injuries to his frontal lobe. It took twenty-seven months, many doctors, and countless more challenges, but we got there. And, remarkably, we got there while holding on to our joy.

Happiness in Tiny Moments

Joy is a lasting feeling of happiness residing within our hearts.

For me, happiness happens in tiny, tenderhearted moments of time. It could be glancing over at one of my children and catching their inquisitive eyes, sparking a smile just between us, or a warm flutter within my heart during an affectionate embrace from my loving husband as we start a new day. Happiness is precious moments like these—simple acts of love that inspire so much joy in my heart. They cause a surge of gratitude to stream through my body. A happy experience perpetuates a natural happy-high that lifts me throughout the day. Those moments are stored in my heart, and when I reflect on them, I amplify my joy.

Every moment counts! Don't discount the minutes in between the highlights of your life. Sometimes, standing on the sideline of some big event creates the most meaningful moments of all. It's those in-between moments that give us the greatest opportunity to reflect and expand our enlightenment. We grow the most when we step away from the spotlight to rest for a moment on the sidelines of our life. It's in these interludes that our resting thoughts unearth profound enlightenment.

One of my most sincere in-between moments was literary a snapshot in time. My friend Anand is a photographer who graciously takes photos of me for my social-media accounts, which I use to share encouragement via my life-coaching business. My daughter, Sienna, loves to come along on these photo shoots, and we enjoy posing for some mother-daughter photos, as well as getting some beautiful photos of her.

We met Anand one particularly cold morning in December, and he captured one photo in particular that means the world to me. It's a black and white photo of yours truly as I stood in my stockinged feet, holding a black pair of high heels. I had lent Sienna my boots for her shot. I was mesmerized in a trance of love as I admired my beautiful girl, enjoying her moment in front of the camera. Although it wasn't *my* moment, I felt a bright light of joy in my spirit, and shining outward—a light of love that only a mother can feel for her child. Anand quickly snapped a picture of it, capturing the love on my face as I stood on the sidelines. It was such a profound and precious moment in my life. It reminds me to cherish each moment— especially those on the sidelines and in-between bigger events. Hold on just as tightly to these moments of joy.

Happiness Is like Riding a Bicycle

Think of happiness like riding a bicycle. You've set out on your journey with a set destination in mind, planned a direct route to arrive in the shortest length of time, and are now happily rolling along. You're anticipating smooth sailing, with no concern for traffic or other obstacles. You don't needlessly worry about a flat tire slowing you down, or any other type of setback that could cast a negative cloud over your excursion.

Now, if a negative set back *does* pop-up, it will have an effect on your happy-go-lucky adventure, briefly slowing you down. But the faster you act to fix the situation, the less you dwell on the setback. The quicker you act, the sooner you can get going on your journey again, moving closer to your destination.

Few of us venture often off the smooth, unobstructed surface of the road intentionally, yet we can let life's setbacks or challenges permanently distract us from moving forward at all. We need to be as quick at recovering from life's setbacks as we would be fixing a tire or rerouting around an obstacle to resume a positive direction on our journey. We've only got a limited amount of time on earth. Don't let negativity slow you down or stop you in your tracks. Your time is too precious to stay stalled in the problem. Instead, focus on the solution and ride towards your destiny.

You Have the Power to Manifest Joy

Joy is a self-manifested state of happiness. If happiness is to last for an eternal period, *internally*, it then becomes joy. Joy is the happiness that rests in your heart. It isn't based on an individual event or experience. Happiness . . . is.

It's often a reaction to a single event or experience. The old English root of the word *happiness* originates from *hap,* meaning *to happen upon,* like a lucky break. It's closely related to happenstance, which is a blend of happen and circumstance, like when someone stumbles into a situation. All this relates to the idea that happiness is conditional upon favorable conditions. Joy differs in many ways from happiness, but I believe the most important note is that *anyone can self-manifest joy in any moment.* You do not need to be in the middle of a happy happenstance. You can use previous happy moments to conjure joy. And you can do this for yourself. You are the only person who can drive the power of joy in your life.

Joy Both Strengthens and Requires Strength

Joy strengthens your heart. Joy gives a calm resilience against the negativity that tries to sway, discourage, or even distract you from achieving your dreams. Joy encourages you to rise up and focus on what brings you happiness. You need to choose joy, even though it's not always easy, because being a joy-seeker will help you discover peace.

It's easy to focus our thoughts on the negative side of life, and much harder to make a conscious choice to seek joy, developing an understanding of what triggers your strength to keep going, and to proactively keep positivity front and center in your life. But by doing so, you can deploy joy to preserve positivity in your own thinking. You can use joy as your own personal, positive-mindset tool kit to combat negativity—a tool filled with joyful memories, joyous thoughts, and the honest intent to seek joy.

Joy is in all of us. We always have the opportunity to set joy in motion within our hearts, within our thoughts, and within our inner soul. When you need strength, you can draw on the energy of joy. At any given point, you can refuel your thoughts and inspire your soul with joy. Or you can use joy's strength to wrestle self-defeating thoughts of negativity into submission. The choice is yours, and I think you'll agree that it's a simple one.

Simple Steps to a Remarkable Life

Simple doesn't always equal easy, but it's a place to start. Simple tips and tools applied to your everyday life can help boost your spirits. It only takes a few minutes a day for you to take heed of what brings you the most happiness, and these happy triggers can be stored away to help you create joy in any moment. Consistency is key in creating this stash of joy-manifesting memories and ideas! It takes commitment to consistently follow the tips in this practical guide to joy. Openly accept these simple concepts—let them seep deeply into your consciousness.

Simply be mindful and aware of what truly makes you jump for joy. Immerse your mind in a plethora of happy thoughts and actions that facilitate the powerful energy of joy, and I promise that joy will start to strengthen your spirit. Your journey through life will become even more remarkable with the power of joy. Accept joy into your life, then get ready for it to shine bright in remarkable ways!

Simple steps towards a remarkable life are easier when we consciously apply joy to *our everyday routines*. We can create a conscious awareness by being mindful of joy and how it will bring strength to your life. As simple as it may seem, this isn't applied very often.

If everyone in the world applied these ideas, all of them would be living with an abundance of joy. Joy would be the light on their journey. Joy would boost and strengthen everyone's spirit to soar. We'd all be less stressed and more able to see even negative situations in a positive scope. Everyone would be living their best life ever. However, as you know, this isn't the case. Although these simple steps can be taken by anyone, not many people are mindful enough—or committed enough—to seek out joy. But you are reading this book, so I know you are different.

Journaling for Joy–

A journal of joyful moments is a great, simple tool to connect with what brings you the most joy. Journaling allows you an opportunity to express your feelings and articulate your thoughts. It provides a visual you can draw on at any time to lift, comfort, and strengthen your spirit. As you write, your journal becomes a book of joyful memories to reflect upon.

Since joy is so closely connected to faith, love, peace, harmony, happiness, and gratitude, your journal will capture moments filled with these emotions and so much more, all in one spot, making it easy for you to reflect on those memories and recall those emotions. Creating a journal of joy boosts you up with your own warm, joyful thoughts.

A journal of joy is a tangible tool to help distract you from focusing only on the sorrows and difficulties of troublesome times. When you've been through difficult challenges, it's not easy to let go of the darkness of the situation, even when it's in the past. So, let yourself begin to see the sunshine again by rereading encouraging, positive messages from your journal of joy. Negativity wastes precious time and energy, so write your worries away with a joyful spirit of gratitude. You will feel the clouds of darkness lighten with the light of joy.

Set aside a few minutes each day. Place your journal where you can quickly jot down what brought you the most joy that day. Look forward to capturing joyful moments as treasured time. Never feel bad if you miss a day or two—keep in joy knowing that you're trying your very best.

If feelings of happiness are conditional based on what is happening around you, achieved only when all the boxes are checked off and everything exterior in life is set up for you to feel good, then start breaking down this dependency. Begin a lasting journey with joy today, and joy will lead you to the open and abundant life you deserve. Feel the light of love in your heart and peace in your soul each day by embracing joy—even the littlest moments of joy each day.

Healthy, Natural Highs

As you journal, you'll discover that happiness, and therefore joy, comes from the inside out. Here are some healthy ways to produce a natural high of happiness in your life from the inside out:

Endorphins

Endorphins are a chemical within the brain, and the release of endorphins makes us happier, calmer, and healthier. It's just one more important benefit to maintaining a healthy lifestyle. The well-known "runner's high" that is felt after lengthy, vigorous exercise is due to an increased release of endorphins.

Below are some simple tips to naturally increase endorphins:

Exercise

Instead of just sitting around, waiting for happy situations to come along, get your body moving to increase levels of endorphins. Exercising also distracts you from waiting or worrying.

Give

Helping others, volunteering, or donating releases these feel-good endorphins to flurry through your body, boosting your thoughts. Giving is a gift of joy for yourself while simultaneously putting a smile on someone else's face. It's a generous way to generate more endorphins.

Spice It Up

It's been said that variety is the spice of life, so why not add a zest of endorphins by savoring some spicy foods. Spicy foods create a stimulus similar to pain in the mouth, which can connect us with an increase in endorphins. Spice your way to a happier life in every season!

Mindfulness

Quiet your mind—calm your thoughts by taking mini-mental-health breaks throughout your day. Joyful moments, meditation, and yoga all trigger endorphins. So, say "yes, please" to mindfulness and namaste away your day. Use these mindful activities to increase the amazing, positive, enhancing endorphins in your body, releasing the power of joy and happiness in your life.

Dark Chocolate!

Numerous scientific studies suggest that eating dark chocolate can boost endorphin levels. Cocoa powder and chocolate contain chemicals called "flavonoids" that appear to be beneficial to the brain. I'm experiencing a joyful moment just thinking about it—a win/win for the happy factor and chocolate lovers in life. As a chocolate lover myself, I'm happy serving you such a sweet treat of joyful information—harmonious balance at its best!

And last but not least, my personal favorite:

Staying One Step Faster Than Fear

When anxiety or worry race through my mind, I hop on the treadmill to quite literally outrun them, while at the same time adding a boost of bliss to pull me back on a happier trail with positivity and possibilities! Running provides me with a quick outlet to release anxious energy. It also gives me an opportunity to boost my happy factor by triggering the awesomeness of endorphins. So, I physically outrun my worries to win the race against stress and anxiety. The heavier the worry, the faster I run. If mind-space was a running track, my worries would be quickly disqualified and disappear from the track!

Serotonin, Dopamine and Oxytocin

Serotonin, dopamine, and oxytocin are also powerful players in lifting our happiness levels, with many parallel benefits to endorphins. These three naturally occurring chemicals start in our brains and impact every part of our bodies. They're often referred to as our "happy hormones." Everyone has the ability to increase levels of these three hormones to combat depression, anxiety, chronic pain, etc.

Positive thoughts can spike our serotonin levels. It's the process of feeling happy by taking the time to focus on joyful memories. Award-winning medical doctor, Dr. Susan Biali Haas, has a life passion for equipping people with the knowledge, skills, and tools to live better lives. Dr. Biali outlines these three happy hormones and neurotransmitters, and their function, in her article, "Happy Hormones and How to Boost Them Naturally," for *Reader's Digest Best Health* magazine.

Serotonin

Serotonin's influence on mood makes it one of several brain chemicals that are integral to your overall well-being—regulating your mood naturally. When your serotonin levels are normal, you feel happier and calmer.

Dopamine

This is the chemical that mediates pleasure in the brain. It's involved in reward, motivation, memory, attention, and even regulating body movements. (When dopamine is released in large amounts, it creates feelings of pleasure and reward, which motivates you to repeat a specific behavior.) Food, sex, and several drugs of abuse stimulate a dopamine release in the brain. Even scrolling on your favorite social media outlet can trigger your brain to release this powerful chemical, leaving you craving more.

Oxytocin

This neurotransmitter has been referred to as "the love hormone." Researchers from Claremont University in California have said that Oxytocin is observed as a bigger influencer of happiness in women than in men. With actions of kindness, nurturing, and sharing your feelings all being ways to prompt an increase in oxytocin, this hormone preforms differently in the male and female amygdala. This is the part of your brain responsible for emotion, motivation, and reward.

Even giving hugs is an easy way to release these happy hormones. If you are smitten with someone, your brain releases dopamine, you get a boost in serotonin levels, and oxytocin develops. You feel a flow of happiness and a rush of positive emotions. So, go ahead don't hold back. Snuggle up to someone you love and trigger happiness today!

Seriously, why not start increasing your happy factor via love? Loving encounters boost oxytocin to flow freely within your body, which sparks a feeling of happiness. Happiness and love are a winning combination! Look for ways to engage a feeling of love. This might be by simply taking time to indulge in listening to your favorite music, or spending time with your furry, lovable companions. I get a surge of happiness by spending a moment with one of my three fur-babies: Teddy Bear and Blu Bear (our adorable Chow Chows) and Princess Leia (our family's beautiful Persian rescue cat). They all lift my levels of happy hormones.

Activities such as nature walk, meditation, or taking a relaxing bath all relieve stress by calming your mind and naturally increasing your happiness. Do whatever works best for you to trigger your happy hormones, and in the process, remind yourself that you are most certainly worthy of amazing amounts of happiness!

Hold on to happiness and you'll encourage joy to resonate in your everyday life. This will help you embark on the journey towards happily ever after, which doesn't need to be exclusive to fairy tales. A queen can look exactly like you! Honor yourself like a queen by taking time to be mindful of what brings you the most joy. Happy times shift into magical, lasting moments of joy.

So, indulge in activities that make you feel happy to perpetuate a feeling of joy. Let joy bring you a *real-life* happily ever after. It will feel incredible, and it will ripple out in ways you might never expect.

Chapter Two
The Ripple Effect of Joy

*"When you do things from your soul, you feel a river
moving in you, a joy."*
– Rumi

Understanding how the power of joy increases your overall happiness is a concept as simple as the above quote from Rumi, the famous thirteenth century Persian poet who is still, today, known as the best-selling poet in the United States.

Rumi thinks of joy as a river. To me, if feels like the light of love. Joy releases a light of love out into the world. Whenever you spread love, you will inevitably receive a beam of joy back. Lead with love to cultivate joy and empower yourself to joyously succeed in all areas of life. Let your heart soak up the light of joy, much like a flower transforms the rays of sunlight to flourish, bloom, and grow. You deserve to thrive with the limitless power of joy. Everyone is worthy of an intimate experience with joy, I hope you enjoy every moment as you discover new ways to connect with joy on your journey.

Let's think about some of those moments. Imagine grabbing your favorite latte. The barista brews you a cup of joy, and while you savor every sip, thoughts of gratitude bring about a joyful moment. Perhaps you "pay it forward" by secretly buying the drink for the person behind you in line. This further ignites the energy of joy to ripple throughout the day. Or, maybe, the all-empowering energy of joy seeps deeply into your heart as you cast out a carefree smile to greet the world, and a gleeful grin beams back in your direction from every kindred spirit who shares in the same delights of the day. A happy-go-lucky vibe unites each of you by way of a sincere smile with no strings attached—just an act of love inspiring joy shared between the kindhearted. Joy ripples alongside love.

You boldly step out into the world with the steadfast energy of joy, born from love, compassion, and a genuine regard for others. Spreading joy adds a layer of love, insulating your heart while at the same time adding a comfy-cozy feeling that strengthens your soul. You feel joy as an act of love that warms even the coldest days of discouragement. You're encouraged to diligently act on joy with deliberate intention, activating its powerful energy, so that you can reap the bountiful victories joy claims for you.

Opportunities for joy surround us all. Joy is as simply as a smile, holding the door open for someone, giving a compliment, or saying hello to an unexpected stranger as you maneuver through your day. The more you are giving of joy, the more joy will become an integrated part of your life. Joy ripples back and forth, and the ripple effects benefit us all. I'll bet that reflecting on these types of joyful encounters gives you a surge of joy right here in this very moment. Hip, hip, hooray! There is more love in the world when we lead with joy every day!

Reflecting Joy

This ripple effect occurs thanks to our beautiful brains. In your brain, you have mirror neurons that subconsciously make you copy the thoughts, emotions, actions, and behaviors of other people. And it works both ways. If you are a source of positivity, joy, and love, the person you are interacting with is likely to assume that behavior as well, and start exuding positivity, joy, and love. Being aware of other people's feelings is an innate human response, which encourages empathy and more love.

The ripple effect of joy works the same way, with a chain reaction of mirroring one another's energy of joy. Simply by engaging in acts or thoughts of joy, others around you will pick up on those emotions and reflect them back. You'll pick up on their joy and reflect *that*, and so on and so on, channeling joy throughout to the world, one reflected connection at a time.

Modeling Joy for Our Children

The ripple effect of joy is especially important for parents and mentors to younger generations. We need to build our children a platform for success that includes understanding how to accept the energy of joy into their hearts to strengthen their spirits.

As a society, it's vital we all contribute to optimizing positivity and prosperity in future generations. Since the mirroring of neurons works the same with all types of energy—positive, negative, or anything in between—our children emulate whatever energy we display in our own behavior. So, the work must begin within ourselves, by making the decision to live with more joy. Let's continually try our best to reboot the youth of today with a positively charged future.

Andrew N. Meltzoff, from the Department of Psychology at the University of Washington, further supports these ideas in his article "Born to Learn," which was published in a paper by his university. In it, he says, "Learning is to behavioral psychology what brain plasticity is to the neuroscience. Not surprisingly, we have evolved a special and very powerful form of learning. That special form of learning is 'imitation,' the ability to learn behavior from observing the actions of others." This is especially true in our relationships as we mentor our children. Simply stated, we need to model the behavior we want to see in our children.

Jeffery and I have been mindful to lead our family with love and courage, even when faced with so much uncertainty. And I think it's paid off. All three of our beautiful children have won citizenship and "student of the year" awards, treasuring two accolades each during their first two years in a new school! It is a remarkable feat and a matter of pride, which has honored our family and created great joy for us. In turn, it has reinvigorated us to lead our kids to adopt the same energy of love, which activates a ripple effect of joy in all our lives, helping us to thrive.

Let's set our sights high in being exemplary role models for younger generations. Let them shine with success by imitating our actions, mirroring our positive energy, and standing strong in their values. All of this will inspire key social development, creating prosperity for us all. We rise higher by helping others.

Be an Ambassador of Joy

Be an ambassador of joy simply by declaring yourself an official role model, and see the rippling of joy through the world. You possess the inner strength and ability to raise awareness by leading others with love and demonstrating what it looks like to journey through life with joy.

You can amplify the effect of your ambassador role by freely giving out praise. Praise is a powerful tool to establish a feeling of worth. When someone feels valued, they get a sense of pride. Pride leads to self-acceptance, which boosts their thoughts to soar with self-love. If social media can manipulate impressionable young minds and leave them feeling little self-worth and low self-esteem, then imagine the impact we, as role models and ambassadors, can have. Let us band together to encourage these beautiful, impressionable young minds to recognize their awesome and amazing gifts.

It's important to stay closely connected with our young people, working hard to offset any reluctance or self-doubt that may come up for them. We need to counteract feelings that they don't measure up, or are less than whole, challenged with a depleted self-worth, by encouraging each and every one of them and equipping them with the power of joy.

Spring into action with simple acts of kindness to lift and inspire someone else's day, making it shimmer with joy. Be mindful of the energy you project on social media and the accounts you interact with online. Eager, impressionable eyes, young and old alike, are watching to emulate all. Initiate the ripple effect of joy, deepening your personal attitude of gratitude, faith, and love, while also strengthening your kinship with others.

Joy creates a harmonious balance for everyone who boldly believes in its infinite possibilities. Empower the world by spreading joy, like wildflowers, in everything you do and everywhere you go. I promise you will witness the vibrant colors of life come alive as love and joy ripple through our world.

Shift your thoughts and you'll shift your future. Negative thoughts often keep us from achieving our full potential. When you shift your thoughts to positive aspects and encouraging affirmations, you change the game by becoming your own cheerleader, and leading others down the same rippling pathway of success.

The Law of Attraction

One simple way to cheer yourself on in life and make things easier is by claiming what you want through your thoughts, and owning those thoughts and intentions as your truest story. The law of attraction says that like always attracts like, meaning whatever you focus on will be exactly what you attract back into your life. The law of attraction is like a boomerang action on your energy. Whatever energy you release out into the universe boomerangs back at you with the same intention.

Out of countless definitions available, I want to share that of best-selling American author and motivational speaker Jack Canfield, as he so clearly explains how it works. He says, "Like attracts like. If you are feeling excited, enthusiastic, passionate, happy, joyful, appreciative, or abundant, then you are sending out positive energy. On the other hand, if you are feeling bored, anxious, stressed out, angry, resentful, or sad, you are sending out negative energy. Your energy frequencies need to be in tune with what you want to attract in your life."

I love how Canfield articulates the law of attraction in an easy way that encourages us to explore what energy we want to attract in our life. He simply tells us that if you want to attract more love and joy into your life, then turn up vibrational frequencies of joy and love.

One amazing experience I had with the law of attraction began as a fun thing I would say jokingly to my close friends and family. In 2014, our family had an incredible year of growth. We were thriving. I wanted to maintain this momentum into the upcoming year, so I declared that 2015 would be "The Year of Kelley," and that our family's good fortune would exceed our stellar year in 2014. Well, 2015 proved to be exactly that. It *was* the Year of Kelley: I enjoyed an abundance of good fortune, and it was our best year ever as a family. Amazing financial security and travel opportunities fell at my feet, and as a family, we enjoyed so many unexpected blessings. It was truly an extraordinary year.

Joy in All Seasons

Joy isn't just for Christmas or exclusive to special celebrations. The energy of joy can deliver a powerful kick of positivity, raising your spirit, every day of the year. Holding on tightly to joyful moments enables us to feel as happy as a holiday, whatever season were in!

That said, it's no coincidence the word "joy" pops up absolutely everywhere you turn during the merriest season of the year. The phrase, "Joy to the world" is synonymous with Christmas cheer over the holiday season for very good reason. At this time of year, the warm, fuzzy feelings of peace, love, and *so* much joy rise up within our souls. We experience a triumphantly joyous celebration as we unite with loved ones on this festive occasion.

The truest meaning of Christmas is a story of love that warms your heart. It demonstrates an immaculate love that beams the energy of joy brightly out into the universe, as God sent his baby son, Jesus, to be a joyous savior for us all. The bible tells us, "An angel of the Lord said unto them, Fear not: for behold I bring you good tidings of great joy, which shall be to all people." – Luke 2:8-14 (New Revised Standard Edition).

This is great joy indeed—beautiful words for believers to embrace as their ultimate ideal, while also elevating our faith.

Christmas is a time of the year when most of us who actively invest in avenues of love are continually self-generating joy. We are more mindful and more consciously aware of self-regulating a joyous state of mind. We are actively seeking the *feeling* of joy. These joy-seeking intentions and actions streamline our blissful thoughts and establish a direct cause-and-effect dynamic. We manifest higher levels of joy, and joy flourishes. Simple acts of joy, like giving or sending salutations of holiday cheer, the excitement of wrapping gifts for loved ones, and spending time together snuggling by the fireplace, or listening to your favorite Christmas songs, all encourage a more joyful spirit.

We possess the same power to tap into this resource of joyful energy all year long. While we might not have the opportunity to make snow angels in summer, no one can stop you from experiencing this "holiday style" of joy on a day-to-day basis. If it's your choice to manifest joy at Christmas, it's just as easily your choice to tap into the power of joy all year long. Cheers to good tidings, each and every day!

Joy Sparks Opportunity

You truly deserve the opportunity to experience joyful moments every single day. You are in the driver's seat of your life and can *accelerate* your joy. Seek simple ways to reframe your thoughts and actions with a positive outlook to increase joy in your life. Start this process by simply being aware of what brings you the most joy. This awareness will nurture a calm energy on your journey. It will help you disengage from worry and stop the cycle of stress from re-emerging in your life.

There are always many sides to a story. Take stress, for example. There are healthy levels of stress that actually work in our favor, for example, the stress that acts as a key element to survival. When faced with extreme challenges, our fight-or-flight response kicks in, adrenaline surges, and it pumps us full of energy to get through the situation. However, living each day with high levels of stress has the opposite effect on the body.

It weakens your immune system, thanks to the high blood pressure that comes along with it. Depression, anxiety, and stress pile on, and absolutely don't make a challenging situation any better. Mindful moments throughout your day help you to de-stress and relax, one moment at a time, while adding a sense of peace, calm, and clarity as you move forward throughout your day.

Your body can react to stress even when you are readily seeking joy. Oh, the joys of trauma! About eight months after Jeffery's traumatic brain injury, I realized I was losing a lot of hair, although I didn't think much of it at the time. Months later, my hair stylist was very concerned that I might be balding (which is not something any of us want to be worried about—especially us ladies)! A dermatologist specializing in hair loss identified my concern as a condition called telogen effluvium, a common cause of temporary hair loss characterized by an abrupt onset of hair shedding several months after a triggering event. In my case, you could take your pick of stressful, triggering events, from Jeffery's initial injury to the many challenges that followed.

Jeffery's accident happened on December 18, 2016. It was a long road to recovery. Through the grace of God's goodness, he is now back, thriving at life, but the years following his injury were tough, and compounded by more tragedy for our family. Two months after his injury, our beautiful aunt Karen received the devastating news that she had stage-four lung cancer. She was a non-smoker. She was also one of my most favorite people, and sadly passed away just over a year later.

In February 2017, my best friend, Kristianne, devastatingly lost her husband, the father of her two beautiful sons, to cancer. He was just forty. In the summer of 2017, my sister-in-law, Amanda, received a devastating diagnosis of colon cancer, which is extremely rare for a forty-year-old woman. Thankfully, the tumor was removed, and she is doing well. After Amanda's diagnosis, my dear step-mother-in-law, Coleen, was diagnosed with progressive supra nuclear palsy (PSP), a rare and aggressive neurological disease. We sadly lost her precious life much sooner than we could have imagined, in May 2019.

Along with developing heart palpitations, the hair loss was one way my body reacted to the increased levels of stress in my life during this time. Outwardly, I was able to refocus my energy on positivity and joy to feel like I was thriving, not merely surviving. Yet, there was a constant stream of stress invading my subconscious via the negative energy that invaded my emotions during this time of turmoil. Heck, just one of the many tragic life experiences from those years would be enough to send someone's heart racing.

Now, I am very grateful that my hair is slowly and steadily regrowing. Hallelujah! I'm also grateful that my heart palpitations have dramatically decreased as time distances me from the many layers of stress once so present in my life.

Take control where you can! I couldn't control the stressful energy coming at me, but I did control my conscious reaction. It made a difference to how I view that season in my life. I was a warrior, not a victim. Some side effects of stress weren't going to stop me from moving towards my best life ever—in any season.

You are the only one who can make joy and peace a priority in your life, whatever you are facing in this season. A positive mindset takes a conscious commitment as you make the choice to follow through with something important. Make a conscious choice to reframe your challenges into something positive. Stay in a joyous state of mind *on purpose*. Be conscious of the energy you are sending out into the universe. It's the energy that boomerangs back at you!

Chapter Three
Warrior Spirit

"Joy is a decision, a really brave one, about how you are going to respond to life."
– Wess Stafford

While in each moment of life, faith is all we truly need, there will be moments when faith is all we've got. (And again, I am not speaking necessarily about faith in a Christian God, but rather in whatever it is that resonates with each of us.) But that's okay, because when all we have left is faith, it ignites our warrior spirit to let us become so much more than we ever could have imagined. Faith ignites the power of joy, strengthening it within us—especially during the most demanding days of our life. Amidst our greatest fears, faith strengthens our inner soul, bringing to existence a warrior spirit.

Initially, my inner warrior ignited from a passion to protect my family when we were faced with a sudden season of escalating uncertainty, a continuum of chaos, initiated by a life-altering disruption in a single moment in time. Jeffery's traumatic brain injury appeared out of nowhere and with absolutely no warning. We had no idea where it would take us next. It was a hard-hitting sucker-punch that left us gasping for air as we barely knew what hit us. Every certainty I felt in my life was extinguished in that one fleeting moment. A new beginning emerged just as quickly, as if we'd walked through a portal into a foreign land. In an instant, our family seemed to be in an alternate world where everything around us looked the same, yet everything was different.

After I picked myself back up from the confusion and disbelief, an inherent, survivalist reaction kicked in, and I was ready to fight back. And while I didn't exactly recognize what was happening within me at the time, in reflection, I realize that a warrior spirit rose up within my soul to exude insurmountable strength—a strength that saw me through a spiraling season of continual concern. It became crystal clear what I needed to do to hold my family together.

Using My Warrior Spirit

One of the toughest steps in holding our family together happened about six months after Jeffery's injury. We were finally connected with a neurosurgeon. While no direct action could be taken, we were still grateful, and the doctor was very supportive. This brain specialist became like a counselor, guiding us through the many slow, unsteady stages to recovery.

He was always encouraging Jeffery and I not to get ahead of ourselves in the healing process, and reminding us that there's no true predictor of recovery time with a brain injury. Time and patience were our best course of action, which wasn't exactly what we wanted to hear. It was very challenging news; however, we maintained a warrior stance. We embraced each day with the faith that, one day, Jeffery's symptoms would subside enough to resume his active life.

One piece of the surgeon's advice that initially turned my stomach was that we should seriously consider our long-term financial plan. We did end up taking this suggestion quite literally, however, given the uncertainty around how long it would take Jeffery to recover. The doctor gave us numerous examples of people in the same situation who'd lost their homes due to an extreme loss of finances as the direct result of the injury.

We knew our savings would not sustain us indefinitely; so, as quick as taking off a bandage (and it stung like a killer bee!), we made the gut-wrenching decision to sell our new, beautiful, shiny, ultra-modern, west-coastal-style dream home. While in-between houses, the five of us cozied up for four months in one hotel room. We bought a fixer-upper, and stayed in that hotel room during renovations on our new place. This was the only affordable option to truly lessen our financial commitment and allow Jeffery the grace to heal.

Another big consideration in our move was continuity for our kids. We wanted them to stay in the same school district at the same school, as they had only been there for less than a year. Even though we remained within the district, I had to petition the school board to gain permission for the kids to continue at their school, as we had apparently crossed a hair-line boarder within the district that brought us closer to another school.

Given the nature of our situation, the principal was willing to stretch the rules and allow the kids to stay. Yay! We celebrated all the victories along the way. It wasn't an easy time, but a warrior spirit must commit to doing whatever it takes to fight through it, so that is what I did.

A Warrior in Warfare

The definition of warrior by the *Merriam-Webster Dictionary* is a person engaged or experienced in warfare (broadly speaking). Warrior is also defined as a person engaged in some struggle or conflict. I can easily identify with the latter part of this definition.

I am a warrior spirit. My warrior spirit nourished an unwavering courage and confidence that encouraged an intrepid mindset—a bravery that would become a transcending light shining brightly, even through the darkest clouds of despair that drifted over our lives to disrupt our peacefulness and any thoughts of joy. Warrior on.

Maintaining a sense of control during chaotic circumstances has little to do with what is going on around us and everything to do with what's happening within our inner spirit. A warrior spirit gives rise to an inner strength we are all equipped with.

A Warrior Does Whatever It Takes

Our warrior spirit adapts, becoming whatever we need it to be in that very moment. And for me, during those difficult days, any resemblance of a "normal life" was comforting. While life felt flawed, I still managed to carry myself with poise, as the fabulous fashionista I am. My personal persona prevailed regardless of the shattering events splintering my life. When I looked my best, I felt better-equipped to tackle the day.

Circumstances had already taken so much from my life. I wasn't going to let them take my style too! So, armed with bold, bright-pink lipstick, pink highlights, a designer purse, and matching shoes, I battled through each day looking fabulous, even though my life was completely flawed.

Vanity isn't always vain. It's quite the contrary. These little niceties became necessities in fostering my warrior spirit. The niceties helped me feel normal in a bazaar new world, while further helping me maintain a bit of pride through a very humbling set of events. With them, I felt stronger as I stepped out to face the battles of the day. I highly recommend you do whatever it takes to boost your day with a little joy, in spite of everything else going on in your life. Those of us feeling flawed by life still have the right to look fabulous.

My values and resilience innately led me to adopt a warrior mindset, which inspired strength and courage to blossom within my inner spirit, and played a key role in keeping my faith strong and my spirit calm throughout an otherwise turbulent set of circumstances surrounding my life. I did this by staying in the moment, as much as possible.

A warrior spirit adheres to a *present-moment mindset,* using each new moment as a tool to achieve an increased sense of control, thus gaining a greater sense of peace within any situation that pops up. Inner peace moves us through life's challenges with more ease, contentment, and joy, and less stress and anxiety. Less stress and anxiety will free up energy to further build on your warrior spirit, shifting your focus from the problem. Instead, you'll recognize that every situation possesses a pathway to a solution. Stopping part way won't give you the end resolution you desire. You must progress through to the end to see the solution.

By focusing my energy directly in the moment, I was able to gain fragments of autonomy while also capturing snippets of control where permitted, which rebooted a sense of calm—a calm that helped me reclaim power back into my life.

Since most stress and anxiety comes from fear or feeling like you have no control, regaining control and focusing your thoughts on the present moment is a key element to fighting stress and anxiety. Keeping your energy focused in the moment, not worried about the past or what's coming up in the future, is the key to thriving—not just surviving—in a challenging situation. This works in the everyday, as well, to boost your spirits and live your best life ever.

Sideswiped

At any given time, we can be abruptly "swept sideways." When life's challenges strike unexpectedly, we can lose our footing. The idea behind being swept sideways is that a quick, overwhelming, and unsteady feeling comes over your life. You feel like you are no longer on solid ground. Being sideswiped can happen to anyone, at any time.

My family's lives had been most definitely swept sideways. Even so, after Jeffery's accident, I continued on as the essence of who I am as an individual. I tried my best to stay 110 percent optimistic, putting faith first with a steady and determined spirit in our new world. Still, challenges tried to swipe me away from my natural optimism.

As we were newly returned from living in the States, Jeffery didn't qualify for provincial healthcare when he received his injury. He also wasn't eligible to receive an exclusive executive healthcare coverage, due to this unforeseen accident happening less than twenty-four hours before a routine, pre-scheduled assessment for an executive-compensated insurance plan. Given Jeffery's stellar health pre-injury, he surely would have been approved at that appointment and received full and complete coverage. But the accident happened only hours *before* his appointment, so we barely received the minimum compensation possible.

In traumatic brain injuries, it can be tricky to determine the depth of injury, and insurance companies readily take advantage of this fact, preying like vultures and discarding their victims for dead. We were faced with insurance representatives who ignored endless industry specialists, doctors' documents, and MRI reports that acknowledged bleeding on the brain. The nasty world of insurers tried to discredit Jeffery's authenticity merely based on outward appearance, when all his injuries were internal. Shameful evils lie within greed and lack of integrity. This is the reality of the industry. While I readily acknowledge that kind and caring individual do exist in the insurance world—those who genuinely have the best interest of the insurers at heart—I only wish one of these gems would have crossed our path.

Timing is everything, and we barely received the base level of compensation. One insurance company shamefully had Jeffery followed and the other almost did not accept our claim. It's disheartening that brain injuries aren't recognized as readily as broken arms and legs. It's difficult when you have no cast to legitimize your injury to scrutinizing eyes, or a direct path to healing like a cast placed for six weeks' recovery. Yet, we did not complain. Instead, we rejoiced in the fact that Jeffery was still with us, even with bleeding in his brain.

We were completely swept sideways, both metaphorically and physically. Our new circumstances gave way to a fight-or-flight state. We were certainly fighting our fears for any bit of control we could find. We dug our feet deep into the ground and held on tightly for twenty-seven months, until Jeffery recovered from the entanglements induced by the accident. Jeffery warriors through like a true hero—my truest hero. A warrior spirit most certainly gave us the upper hand in the progress of healing and proved vital to our victory.

We'd been swept sideways with only remnants of familiarity remaining. Physically, we all looked the same, albeit nothing else about our lives did. Nothing was similar to the exceptionally blessed life we had enjoyed before Jeffery's accident, simply nothing. My husband had been an extremely successful, award-winning leader in his industry. He was strategic, an extraordinary executive who vibrated with life. He lived to the fullest. And now, my husband suffered each day in pain.

Jeffrey's warrior spirit prevailed stronger and more resilient than ever, though. He was truly a superhero of hope for our whole family. Even after those twenty-seven months of recovery, lingering symptoms like pressure headaches hint at a life once severely sideswiped. Still, Jeffery's extraordinary spirit warriors on to shine bright, honoring himself with pride and a continued determination to live his best life ever. He emits a triumphant glow of victory, knowing he rose above adversity and won. For that, he will be a hero in my heart forever.

A Solution to "Sideswiped Status"

After being swept sideways, we frantically tried to grasp onto anything remotely familiar, hoping to ground ourselves through the uncertainty of our current events. We treaded with caution. We were conscious that the suddenness of our "sideswiping" would not create a constant state of chaos in our minds and take hold of our lives. Our warrior spirits wouldn't allow it.

Chaos could've taken over the calm areas in our thoughts. Chaos leaves little room for individual ideas to surface. A sideswiping action distances us from feeling in control. Our challenges absorb space that would otherwise be given to our individual thoughts, while fear eagerly waits to take over our control. Frozen by our very own fear-based thoughts, "sideswiped status" steals our autonomy and replaces it with fear.

But I wouldn't let this happen. I shifted my energy and redirected my thoughts from focusing on a scary situation. Instead, I focused on faith. I let faith lead me away from my ongoing fears. This is about actively seeking a solution to offset a "sideswiped status" that sets in and tries to control your life. It's not easy. For me, it meant continually refocusing on faith.

Over the past century, many psychologists have studied ways to combat fears. One process is known as "fear extinction." When we are thinking of fear extinction, it means that we need to create a new response to the stimulus that is causing fear in us, so we start associating positive things with our fears, and they begin to feel less frightening.

Don't get swept away by your problems. We might not be able to avoid bad situations in our lives; however, we can absolutely take a strong stand, not letting the challenge sweep all our joys away. Mindset is everything. Sitting in sorrow is sad. We must continue switching our thoughts back to a frequency of faith, especially during the turbulent times in our lives. Otherwise, our biggest fears and greatest sorrows will be crowned the winner in our internal dialogue. Fight back with faith.

The Game of Cat and Mouse

Fear inevitably limits the opportunity of joy. Fear limits our ability to tap into the power of joy, while faith releases joy by creating hope for a brighter tomorrow. Joyful moments strengthen our spirit to shine, especially during the challenging times. Holding onto joy won't be easy, but it will definitely be worth it. Adding joyful moments isn't masking over real-life struggles. Joy is a strengthening tool of resilience to raise your spirit to soar above the sorrows. Joy is like the comfort of a mother's kiss given to her child as she tucks them in snugly for a night of slumber.

In the midst of our road to recovery, a favorite aunt was fighting lung cancer, my best friend lost her husband, my sister-in-law suffered through surviving colon cancer, and my step-mother-in-law lost her life to a devastating disease. Fear invariably lurked throughout my thoughts, eager to eradicate my faithful spirit. It was a cat and mouse game where the cat represented my faith—a majestic stealth-warrior feline ready to pounce on the mouse of fear, who under even slightly normal circumstances would have no chance against the bold, sleek action of faith. In my situation, though, the tiny mouse of fear was present so often that he appeared more like a monster than a mouse. I had to up my cat-woman instincts and actions, my faith like a lioness protecting her pride. We must consciously recommit to our faithful tendencies as many times as it takes, or we risk fear outrunning our faith as it races around to take control of our thoughts.

There are so many unexpected events in life that can sweep you sideways, placing you in a center seat to face your greatest fears. Confront them equipped with a warrior spirit. Embrace each season with courage, no matter how off-course your fears will try to make you feel. When difficulties pop up unexpectedly and start to sweep you sideways, your comfort zone quickly becomes a battle zone. Be brave. Stand strong in the resilient stance of a warrior.

Going through challenges feeling negative and discouraged, driving with fear, will ultimately alter the outcome. The same can be said for facing the situation with faith, optimism, and joy. Keep faith and hold onto your joy, so you won't miss a minute. Reflecting on where my energy could be most useful, and then refocusing it back into the present moment, perpetuated a feeling of peace throughout all those challenges. Maintaining a warrior mindset was vital while exploring new and unchartered situations with each passing day.

Chapter Four
Autonomy

"To be yourself in a world that is constantly trying to make you something else is the greatest accomplishment."
— Ralph Waldo Emerson

Let's take a moment to explore the importance of developing our individual autonomy, and its direct connection to living our best lives. My belief is that personal autonomy is the self-regulating action of voluntarily claiming and owning our direction in life. It's important to understand how to maintain autonomy even under extenuating circumstances. Autonomy can affect every facet of our life, as it involves taking proper self-control to ensure we are making decisions on our own behalf. Autonomy allows us to apply our own thoughts and feelings to protect our interests. You should have the greatest vested interest in your life. Autonomy provides an opportunity for contentment, as you feel more at peace knowing your decisions have been made with your best interests in mind.

Others can't weigh in without biases clouding their judgment. Psychologically, autonomy is an entangled set of attitudes and skills, some of which include the ability to debate with others, to appreciate different points of view, and to reason. And to do all those things, a person needs to have a sense of self-respect, self-worth, and exceptionally powerful feelings of self-love.

In simple words, autonomy means to make choices and hone decision-making skills, be it as a child or as an adult, in workplace decisions or family matters. There are some circumstances in which it's easier to be more autonomous, while others can undermine our personal autonomy. We live life simply by directing ourselves down the path we have selected, even if we believe a *higher power* has designed a master plan for our personal journey, autonomy is a gift of grace to self-govern, an active ability to respond first hand to your own life circumstances.

In as much as we rely on our intuitive senses to guide our steps, utilizing autonomy gives us the freedom to make the final move in the moment.

A *higher power* may decide to override our tendencies or keep them in play as a learning curve for future success, yet we are given an autonomous moment of grace to self-determine our next step.

Make time to reflect on what's important, who truly is making decisions in your life, and how to gain the control you need to move forward towards your best life ever. The decision is indeed yours to make, no matter how persuasive others' pleas maybe to the contrary. Their first interest isn't you, just as yours isn't them.

Autonomy Is Personal Control

Autonomy is about personal control and our independent thoughts and views, free from external forces or influences. Feeling in control is vital to your personal growth. Autonomy means acting without feeling influenced or oppressed by exterior pressures. So, it makes perfect sense that, when turbulent times hit, we feel robbed of the self-regulation and empowerment that autonomy provides. Autonomy plays a key factor in self-development, quality of life, and our vital connection to contentment and peacefulness.

Many sociology and psychology theorist have written different views defining autonomy and how it relates to each factor of our lives. There are at least four varying definitions of autonomy in political and moral philosophy. According to American Joel Feinberg, who was widely recognized as a leading political and social philosopher, autonomy is a "set of rights expressive of one's sovereignty over themselves, a personal ideal, the actual situation of self-government, and the capacity to govern." So, if we are to form an independent theory of autonomy, we can simply say that autonomy is activating our own personal control, making decisions for ourself on our own behalf. While there is still so much to be said and understood around the concept of autonomy, and it may even feel overwhelming at times, it doesn't need to be complicated.

Personal Control is a Basic Human Right

Autonomy is a key tool in achieving a sense of contentment and joy in all areas of life. It's essential to living a happy life. Autonomy is personal control over our life, and a foundation of freedom to foster unlimited growth potential within any given area. Our autonomy undergoes extreme adversity in challenging situations where, generally speaking, the situation prevents us from feeling in control.

Connecting with our autonomy is a basic human right for us all. Fight for your rights. When I am in a situation where my autonomy seems threatened, I start feeling anxious, like my heart is suffocating and won't allow me to breathe as deeply as I'd like. I can get this way in a crowded waiting room at the doctor's office or the DMV. I've discovered over the years that waiting is a big trigger for my feelings of being out of control.

Whenever irrational fears around waiting flood my thoughts, I distract myself by reclaiming the moments with thoughts that bring me joy. For example, I'll quiz myself with questions about my favorite childhood television shows. I may ask myself whether I can still sing the entire theme song to *Scooby Doo* or *The Brady Bunch*. I get so immersed in my pleasant reminiscing that my spiraling-out-of-control feeling diminishes, and I begin to feel less vulnerable and more empowered. This happens simply by refocusing my thoughts towards a positive mindset.

Everything's a process, so give yourself the grace to step forward even when it's not easy. You are absolutely worth it! Truthfully, just now, writing and sharing this example gave me a flutter of anxiousness—and I was merely *reflecting* on the experience of waiting at the doctor's office! Thank goodness for Scooby and the gang. They always seem to be in the right place at the right time to help!

Choosing to Rise Up

Sometimes, our autonomy seems to get sucked into a cyclone effect. Our freedom gets sucked away by our situation, and our situation leads us down a foreign path where troublesome circumstances start to absorb our energy—energy that would have previously been used to reenergize ourselves and our spirit. The cyclone effect is now redistributing energy towards the need to confront each of life's new trials. A sense of chaos arises within us, igniting a frightening feeling that we have lost our control. Losing a sense of our autonomy sinks our spiritual energy, which under normal circumstances, would lift our spirits to soar. Then we sink further into a negative spiral of despair while rapidly losing our autonomy. Rise back up. Regain control and stop the cyclone effect from taking hold of your life.

You need to regain control—regain autonomy—by refocusing your energy into the present moment. A present-moment mindset seems to slow down this autonomy-sucking cyclone by reclaiming the snippets of time and energy lost to challenging events. Direct energy and control back towards yourself by focusing on what you can take control of in that very moment. Don't scatter your energy by focusing on what you can't do. Refine it by focusing on what you *can* do. Simply by being aware of this concept, you will awaken powerful energy in yourself that can draw you back to regaining autonomy. Then you will feel more in control of your life. Activating your autonomy releases an inner freedom for your spirit to soar once more.

As an example, forgiveness activates our autonomy by empowering us to redirect our thoughts towards understanding and empathy for the one who hurt us. Forgiveness unleashes freedom in our heart—the freedom of autonomy to choose a more peaceful path forward with forgiveness, while also prompting the power of joy. Nelson Mandela is famous for his resolution to implement a policy of forgiveness as opposed to revenge when he became the president of South Africa in 1994.

In one of his most famous quotes, from when he was released from prison four years before his presidency, he said, "As I walked out the door toward the gate that would lead to my freedom, I knew if I didn't leave my bitterness and hatred behind, I'd still be in prison." This is an enlightened perspective. This autonomous act released Mandela's spirit to shine, even in the most unjust of circumstances. Directing your thoughts to feel triumphant when little control is apparent in your life is a joyful action of a warrior spirit.

Simple Steps to Regain Control

Here are some simple, although not always easy, steps to regain control through our autonomy. When you are actively, consciously, confidently, courageously redirecting your focus on the present moment, these simple steps do become easier.

1. Empower with Positivity

You need to clearly define the steps to maintain autonomy in situations where you feel little control. Start by empowering yourself with positivity. Positivity sees possibility, and possibility spawns solutions. Solutions create a freeing feeling of control over any situation. Boom! Autonomy is back in the house.

2. Stay Present

Stay present in the moment. A present-moment mindset is a powerful tool to empower autonomy. Don't dwell in the past or fret about the future. That wastes precious energy and doesn't aid in finding a solution for any difficult circumstance. A present-moment mindset will help you recapture control in your life. Meditate in the moment.

3. Practice Self-Love

Remind yourself that you're totally and completely lovable. Don't let doubt or self-sabotage leave you surrendering as the victim. Reclaim control with positive self-talk and positive affirmations about yourself, and be victorious in your life.

4. Reframe and Refocus

Reframe and refocus energy onto what you have immediate control over. You can also create a quick list of immediate and achievable goals as a safety net for success. Write the list down, even if it's just a reminder to be positive or to simply breathe deeply, and you're more likely to remember it. Do whatever you can to gain the confidence you need to stay in control. You've got this!

5. Expect the Unexpected

We spoke earlier in the chapter about self-acceptance. Now, shift to accepting each new situation in your life. You don't have to like a situation, but denying what's happening won't make it go away.

Believe me; I've tried! Accepting your current situation, simply by not resisting it, will help you hold on to your autonomy. And yes, I completely understand that this is easier said than done; however, to state this simply: Resisting change makes challenging circumstances much more challenging!

Change is constant, while resistance is futile. You are not your "problem," so accept that sometimes you won't have complete control over everything in your life. And as strange as it may sound, when we release anxious feelings of stress or useless thoughts of worry from our mind, it actually clears room for an increased sense of autonomy. So, focus on what you *do* have control over, in that very moment, by refocusing your thoughts on what you *can* control.

This is one of my most coachable areas, and one that I am very passionate about.

Had I not acted on the principles of autonomy during my extended, agonizing season of sorrow, I would be sitting in a corner somewhere, sucking my thumb, and not writing this guide encouraging you! I kinda like writing this book, so I'm super happy I chose to act on my autonomy instead of sitting in sorrow, feeling defeated. That's not to say I didn't have my bouts of ugly crying. Of course, I did. But I always picked myself up again and directed myself back to feeling in control, even if it was only for a moment, reflecting on something that brought me joy.

Using Joy to Regain Autonomy

We always have the choice to explore joy to lift our spirits. Even now, I embody a feeling of empowerment as I reflect on a joyful moment during a season of seemingly endless challenges in my family's lives. Yes, there were moments of joy, even though a cyclone effect was in full throttle, relentlessly sucking our autonomy aside, and I felt control was spiraling away from my reach. I still had moments meditating on the magnificent hummingbirds at my feeder, for example, and a few seconds of joy directed fragments of control back into my world.

Directing yourself towards mindful moments of gratitude, creating a balanced life, living a healthy lifestyle, maintaining a regular fitness routine, and keeping faith all play key roles in generating the power to boost the feeling of being in control. Staying positive and seeking joy throughout all seasons of life will enable you to not lose out on those pockets of time where life gets challenging.

Hold onto joy, even when you feel like your life is under the spiraling effects of a cyclone. Reclaim a feeling of freedom via the powerful energy of joy. Our time on earth is precious. Don't let circumstances steal the minutes away. Take back control of your life by acting on your personal autonomy.

Chapter Five
A Warrior in Faith

"I can be changed by what happens to me. But I refuse to be reduced by it."
– Maya Angelou

The term "warrior mindset" connects deeply to my core values, especially as I think about our family's most challenging season. It truly amazes me how faith lets our true colors shine even brighter in the storm, shimmering with many brilliant colors, all reflecting the resilience to adapt and conquer through adversity. Whether a situation be good or bad, the more faith you emit through your thoughts and actions, the more distinct and brilliant you will shine. The light will come from the many attributes that faith can evoke, like confidence, courage, positivity, resilience, and most certainly joy—all of which are a source of strength.

If these strengths represented the colors of the rainbow, an illuminating, shimmering glow would create a colorful palette so beautiful, so bright, that the whole sky would gleam with a glorious array of faithfulness—the faithfulness of a true warrior spirit. May your inner spirit awaken the brilliance of these colors to gleam boldly, lighting your journey to shine through life as a warrior.

My faith developed through a direct alignment with the Lord, as I remained open and eager to receive signs of encouragement to strengthen my inner spirit. Yours may come from somewhere, something, or someone else. It does not matter.

My faith shone like gold glistening through a beaming ray of light, radiating off the sun, making me feel triumphant within even small feats of victory throughout the day, like landing a specialist medical appointment or staying focused on the hope of healing with little encouragement.

I define a "warrior spirit" as someone who leads with courage and kindness, and is a resilient joy-seeker. It's someone who moves through a challenging situation powered by faith and an unshakable belief in themselves. A warrior spirit adopts strength not from dwelling on fear but by facing their greatest fears with the unbreakable strength of faith.

Many of my most profound realizations are retrospective. I only came to realize I was a true warrior spirit while in a state of reflection. At that time, I completely identified myself as a warrior—a warrior spirit of faith battling beyond my circumstances with courage, resilience, love, kindness, and joy. These attributes acted as symbolic weapons, equipping me with an inner strength and honoring me with the ability to distinguish good within each stormy situation.

Even more directly, I came to consider myself as a "warrior-spirit princess." Adding *"princess"* only strengthens my warrior status. As in every classic princess story, the princess reigns victorious, and victorious is definitely how I feel moving forward beyond my circumstances. Circumstances are continually changing, so don't get left behind, stalled by fear. Continue to move forward *with* the fears. That is what a warrior-spirit princess does.

Faith over Fear

Even a warrior spirit can struggle to find the good in the day. In my family's most troubling times, the good wasn't always apparent, especially as life kept pulling us further sideways. We felt completely derailed at times, but it was our continued faith that lit our path and kept us moving forward. God's light guided us through the depths of our troubles to shine bright amidst the dull, dismal series of events that continuously tried to strike us down. It was a light that always gave us at least a flicker of hope for tomorrow.

What do you have faith in? What guides you and lights your way? Nature? Music? Your own innate strength and sense of humor? Whatever it is, embrace it—embrace that faith—and always hold on to hope.

Maintaining a warrior spirit takes perseverance and a genuine discipline in faith. A warrior spirit means believing in yourself and your ability to get through any situation with an abundance of unwavering faith. A warrior-spirited person makes a *conscious decision* to lead with a faith-over-fear mindset. Warrior spirits innately understand that limitations stem from reluctance and fear-based thinking.

Those who are reluctant to see situations with faith will hinder faith's ability to work. You must first spark possibility in order to overcome obstacles. Possibility is sparked by faith and by believing that every situation has a solution. When possibility and faith are driving your spirit, you begin to uncover solutions. Faith sparks possibility in the same way, by mirroring the attributes of a warrior spirit.

Warrior Faith and Resilience

While doubt will slow down faith's ability to ignite change, fear can be paralyzing. Fear leaves faith at a standstill. When this happens, our *thoughts* must spark and engage in possibility in order to reignite its flame. A warrior spirit's flame of faith will extinguish both reluctance and fear, preventing them from taking root in their spirit.

Enduring the depths of reluctance and fear strengthened my spirit to warrior through adversity. It seemed as though the more adversity that was in my path, the greater my capacity to recover from the difficulties and toughness. A warrior is resilient. You are much more resilient than you think. Never forget your inner powers.

A warrior fights through challenges, coming out stronger on the other side. So, please, don't waste time in worry or fear. There is greatness in your future, for you are a warrior through and through. You possess an inner warrior. Let your spirit flourish by adopting the tools in this book to discover joy through all seasons. Don't simply survive challenging situations. Choose to thrive amidst the challenges, not missing a minute of your precious life. It's a truly brave and courageous decision to take. You've most definitely got this. Warrior on to live your best life ever.

Warrior on with Affirmations

Keep your spirit safe with three positive affirmations: one for courage, a second for faith, and the third to let the power of joy flow directly into your heart. Personalize each affirmation, designing it especially for you, as if you were designing your dreams with these three thoughts. They might even spark a giggle of joy every time you say them. Delight in their intent and empower yourself with their meaning. Write them down or memorize them, so they can always rest in your heart. Then draw on them for comfort or reassurance whenever you feel like you need a lift. These customized thoughts can warm your heart during the most difficult moments, lifting you to conquer every challenge in your life. Use these affirmations to stay positive. Positivity is the driving force. Positivity is my superpower, and it can be yours too.

Empowering Your Warrior Spirit to Shine

Here are some simple tips to empower your warrior spirit to shine. Use them along with your personalized affirmations:

1. Stand stronger than your situation. It may feel like your troubling times have a strong hold over your life, but dig your heels in deeper with the resilient stance of a warrior.
2. Uphold victory by letting go of the role of victim. You have greatness within you. You are a victorious-warrior spirit.
3. Acknowledge and validate your feelings and emotions. Honesty is always the best policy. Don't sweep your emotions under the rug. Be true to how you're feeling. Honor yourself.
4. Evaluate your situation by identifying your emotions—good or bad. Identify what is coming up for you. Look for what might have triggered you to feel this way, then ask yourself what achievable steps you can act on to resolve any underline issues. Reframe discouraging, negative emotions with positive thoughts to find a direct response to challenging emotions.
5. Use faith to combat feeling of fear. Fears come up for us all. It's okay to feel afraid. It's not okay to allow your fears to be the driving force in your life. Faith and determination will inspire you to learn to move past your fears or even move forward *with* fear. Use prayer (whatever that looks like for you) as a powerful weapon to facilitate fear extinction in your thoughts.
6. Have an attitude of gratitude. Positivity sees possibilities, so be your own advocate and ask questions. Get the answers you need to reassure yourself that you're on the right track to be successful. Being proactive in your circumstances, rather than reactive to them, will increase the feeling of control in your life.

7. Focus on the present moment to reduce the stress and anxiety brought on by reoccurring assumptions that are based on patterns of the past or by manifesting false predictions of future threats. Yes, those predictions *are* false, because unless you have a crystal ball, you can't predict the future. So, why not focus on manifesting ideas that will put you on top of the mountain, instead of sinking in quicksand? Warrior spirits are mountain dwellers, and you most definitely deserve top spot! I'll be standing strong beside you!

An Exuberant Intent to Thrive

Imagine this: In evaluating your life, you've checked off each box as exceeding expectations. Life feels like it is exceedingly awesome in every way. Look out world, here you come! We can gain this kind of inner strength and confidence simply by feeling or focusing on an *exuberant intent to thrive*. It makes us feel unstoppable, like optimism is a super power. The world feels like it's at our feet. Happy hormones are generating with every single positive thought. In this state, there are seemingly no wrong moves, as we flow forward freely, like eagles soaring through the sky. It sounds fabulous, right? Sign me up too, please!

The intent to thrive in life is an awesome, natural high. Is this state of euphoria realistic or achievable in any of our lives? I'm most certainly not going to burst our dreamy intent-to-thrive bubble. Believe me, I'm a dreamer, with my thoughts resting in the clouds. I like to think of *thriving* as a state of mind to strive towards. Some people may thrive with an abundance of joy, while others have a different approach to defining what it means to thrive. Either way, it's about our *intent* to thrive. That's what lets us reach new levels in life.

Setting the right intent equips our inner spirit to flourish, so when we believe we can do anything, we usually accomplish whatever we set our determined mind on. This is true even beyond seeking out pathways to explore the energy of joy. We must push past our doubts and fears and shout-out boldly to the universe, declaring our deliberate intention to thrive, while seizing each new opportunity as a victory that illuminates our path. Optimism illuminates our pathway in life to shine, with an exuberant intent to thrive.

The Choice to Thrive

Thriving through adversity is one of the main messages I wanted to spread through this guide. I wanted to share our family's story to debunk limiting beliefs or myths that survival mode is the only option in a trying time. Surviving is a primitive way of living. You always have a choice to thrive. At the time, I chose to thrive by protecting my precious emotions. They were in a frayed and fragile state. I could manage awesome on my own or okay in a small circle of thoughtful people who knew what I was going through, but other than that, I felt it was a challenge to protect myself out in the world.

So, I simply chose not to wear my challenges on my sleeve for all to see, but rather, to privately process each of them. First, I adapted to these new emotions and then evaluated how to move through each new challenge. This calm process strengthened my core self to adopt an "intent to thrive" within any circumstance that popped up.

God gives us the grace of reflection to strengthen our spirit when trudging through murky waters. Honor yourself with the opportunity to reflect on your next move. Give yourself that grace period before leaping into the ocean without grabbing a life preserver. It's easy, amidst the initial chaos, to let well-meaning friends and family get caught up in the mess, yet often they only add to its clutter.

Sort out your feelings first, and the direction you take will be your own. That being said, everyone needs to feel love and support from their circle of friends and loving family. Just make sure your "rock" isn't actually sinking you further down into the despair of your problems. That's my rock-solid advice to keep your sanity. That's what worked for me!

No Sudden Movements

Reacting haphazardly to uncharted territory is dangerous. Moving too quickly distracts you from the solution. If you are deep in a problem, there is no wiggle room to plan a solution. You need your warrior stance to be adaptable by adopting a solution-focused mindset.

Have you ever been suddenly faced with a challenging situation so difficult and daunting that you immediately run for comfort to the first person who pops up on your phone, and then proceed to divulge every detail to them? In your panic-stricken state, you felt like the more people you told, the more support you could rely on—only to discover that you felt *more* isolated than when you first discovered the devastating news and you were the only one who knew.

Pick your peeps carefully through the highs, lows, and in-betweens of life. Taking an attitude of quality over quantity is the safest course of action to protect your heart. We all have those lovable friends and family who feel compelled to share equally heart-wrenching stories from the archives of their own life. You end up listening to their old story (that you've likely heard before), meant to make you feel better, while wasting your precious time and valuable energy focused on them. Yeah, that's helpful!

So, keep your circle small when it comes to pouring out your heart or seeking support through challenging circumstances. I'm not saying you should hide away your heart; just take steps to protect it! Absolutely engage with people who truly have your best interests at heart. To find those people, you need to choose wisely. You deserve an acute listener in your time of need, not a chronic storyteller.

I've learned throughout the years that, most of the time, recounting each draining, dramatic detail of an event is exhausting. Often, the problem gets resolved on its own, but all your worrying and stressing over the situation wore you out more that the pending problem. All your engagement on the issue spotlighted exactly the opposite energy than what you intended to focus on. You wasted time and all your precious energy on something that may, in the end, have solved itself. (I'm talking about micro-events more than the macro-ones, here.) And I bet worrying lent no solution. Or perhaps the situation, luckily, didn't get as bad as you predicted, leaving you to wonder why you'd spent so much time and energy sharing the intimate details of your heart. It may also have left you feeling exhausted and emotionally drained from all the drama. You deserve more!

Processing the situation is your first step. Then evaluate how this challenge will impact your immediate future. After you have done that analysis, equip yourself to work with what you have direct control over in the moment. If that means sitting peacefully, or cleaning the house from top to bottom to keep your idle hands from stressing, then that's the right move for you! Do whatever provides a sense of control over the situation.

I love lying on the sofa, looking out of my window, and watching the birds at my feeders. I literally get lost in the moment. It's a moment of joy that centers me back into the present. I often practice breathing exercises or stand in-front of the window in a yoga pose—maybe tree stance or warrior pose—watching my feathered friends. It's those small moments we create for ourselves that tend to mean the most. Carve out meaningful moments to create a peaceful vibe to strengthen your spirit through all seasons.

Optimism, Realism, and Pessimism

It's the pessimistic peeps who hold the opinion that realism is the opposite of optimism. In fact, we all know that a pessimist's perspective is the true opposite of optimism. The "Negative Nancies" of the world hold their pessimistic perspective on a pedestal, sneakily disguised as realism, when the only thing real is their negative slant on life. They pass themselves off as realists, trying hard to offset the enlightenment of an optimistic mind. If you've ever had someone tell you that you're too optimistic, then you know exactly what I mean. The Negative Nancies position themselves as realists to claim a more positive light from their darker, pessimistic views, but always with a negative undertone in hand. In actuality, a realist approach is quite complementary to optimism.

A *PsycholoGenie* article says that pessimism and realism are very different concepts. It says a pessimist notices negativity more so than positivity, and believes the world is predominantly bad. Optimists, on the other hand, see negative situations as setbacks in the bigger— more positive—picture. It says, "Pessimists refuse to see the good in people and life and are convinced that things are getting worse with every passing day. A realist is someone who will see things for the way they really are."

Whether realists or optimists are the most optimally adjusted individuals is debatable, but either way, both positions offer a valued approach to living your best life. Don't let the skeptics tell you any different! The term "toxic positivity" was most likely coined by a cynical pessimist pleading a negative defense.

Chapter Six
Peacefulness

"I define joy as a sustained sense of well-being and internal peace—a connection to what matters."
– Oprah Winfrey

Inner peace is unique for us all; however, one pathway to achieving a sense of peacefulness remains consistent for everyone. Of course (you guessed it), I am referring to the power of joy. The energy of joy and a feeling of peacefulness go hand in hand. They're like two peaceful, joyful peas in a pod. As distinct qualities, joy and peace are extraordinary phenomena. Together, this incredible duo becomes an unstoppable synergy that provides a sincere source of contentment and a profound feeling of love, when we diligently strive towards them.

Each of us a unique—one of a kind. Everyone is driven by different passions, ideologies, and experiences, which develop our unique pathway to feeling peacefulness throughout our lives. As with joy, achieving a feeling of peacefulness is an inside job. External influences only distract you from a sense of peace. Ultimately, only you can determine whether you live a peace-filled, peaceful life.

ME Moments

I'm always fascinated by observing others' abilities to discover a sense of peacefulness in the moment. My favorite person in the world gives us a great example. Jeffery establishes a peaceful rhythm at the end of his long, intense, daily work schedule in a way that's unique to him and his interests. He will stretch out and get comfy on the couch, iPhone in hand, filing through hundreds of work emails, while catching a UFC match. In this, Jeffery discovers a peaceful moment unique to him. It delights me to observe this ritual that is ever-calming for him.

Jeffery gives himself a much-deserved "ME moment" by enjoying something he loves to watch while crushing email. It's a harmonious balance that brings him much peace. A *ME moment* is anything that helps you restore energy—a **M**y **E**nergy moment, if you will. My ME moments differ greatly from Jeffery's, although the result is the same. Discover for yourself what brings you peace in a ME moment. As long as it isn't illegal or immoral, I'll always honor and respect your zen space. Use it to rest your thoughts for a moment or to promote peacefulness—whatever that looks like. Take a ME-tastical moment just for you.

My zen space is chill-axing on our swing bed. It's the ultimate experience in luxury, outdoor comfort, fully-equipped with plush bedding and an electric mattress cover to stay extra cozy on those chilly days when you still want to be outside enjoying a natural setting. It provides me a beautiful moment of relaxation, listening to the birds and all the nature that surrounds me, while snuggled up cozy, swaying gently, enjoying a peaceful moment within my spirit.

Such beautiful memories too! My kids would pile on our floating bed for story time. During the summer months, dusk sparked our backyard to illumination via the twinkling sparkle of fire flies. We might get lucky and gaze out as a grouping of deer passed by, whilst an owl or two could be heard joyfully hooting in the background—all as I read each adventurous tale. Peacefulness provoking joyful moments indeed.

That is the incredible thing about peaceful moments: The experiences are as unique as we are. So, honor yourself by exploring some mindfulness to provide peace in your life.

Peace Will Prevail

Peace is a truly remarkable asset to us all. Quiet moments of mindfulness top my list for finding peace; however, I can feel a moment of peacefulness in the middle of a busy shopping center or at an amusement park. The place is less important than the emotions that come up for me in that moment. An inner peacefulness can arise when witnessing tender acts of kindness, watching others enjoying time together, or simply by seeing others caught up in joyful moments. Any of these can evoke an inner sense of harmony in my heart that illuminates a peaceful, warm glow in my being.

A celebration in life is more than merely a place to go and party. It's the inner realization that, regardless of your location in life, *peace will prevail*. A state of inner peace is the ultimate prize won by the enlightened spirits who recognize its value. Peace is a precious and profound commodity to capture contentment, joy, harmony, and love, in order to win big at the game of life. Draw on the notion of a peaceful approach any time, or anywhere, to thrive in life.

I live my everyday life in a continuum of reflexes and brief moments of reflection, which let me center myself back into a peaceful state. Daily distraction can be as trivial as waiting in line at the grocery store or as complex as several members of your family being diagnosed with terminal diseases as your husband recovers from a traumatic brain injury. The distractions may be different for each of us, but our reframing back to a peaceful state of mind is exactly the same process.

The external situation that led to discontentment is secondary to understanding what provides us with the staying power of peace. That means it's less about the motivating factor for achieving inner peace and more about living your life aligned with what inspires peace for you. Seek whatever's going to spark peace. Our common goal for inner peace is to feel comfortable and at rest in mind, body, and soul.

Peace Amidst Struggle

Inner peace is most certainly not the absence of struggle. However, our ability to hold on to a sense of peacefulness even while engulfed in the center of a storm is very telling. It tells me your commitment to living your best life is *unsinkable*. It is an unwavering courage only a peaceful spirit can provide. We are consciously aware that discontentment is ready to take control at any moment, but our thoughts and feelings fuel our ability to drive inner peace throughout our life.

Developing a peaceful approach to how you pursue life can be as simple as switching your thoughts to a more harmonious frequency or as challenging as fighting the merciless waves of a typhoon. Once we understand how to engage a peaceful mindset, inner peace becomes one of our most powerful tools for inspiring joy. While you don't often associate peace with a warrior, in the case of cultivating our warrior spirit, peace is a powerful sword of protection—a reliable resource helping you thrive on any occasion. Stream peacefulness through mindful, calming moments where you intentionally breathe or repeat your make-you-feel-happy affirmations. Positive affirmations build a strong alliance with peace. And joy is peace's most kindred ally.

Inner peace sparks joy's strength and energy—and the process works equally as great in reverse. Drawing on moments of joy brings us inner peace, which helps us hold on to our joy and feelings of peace, increasing our resilience and strengthening our spirit.

Honor Yourself with Peace

Simply believing you always deserve joyful moments and a peaceful spirit will equip you with a tool of honor. Honor yourself by not allowing temporary circumstances to steal your inner peace. Remaining peaceful is not circumstantial. Inner peace and joy are *always* within your warrior heart, irrespective of the circumstances.

Everyone is equipped with an innate ability to access inner peace. Claim your power through meditation, positive mantras, and especially by tapping into the power of joy. Grasp a stronghold, and never surrender your peaceful spirit. Negative circumstances don't have to take over your thoughts and steal your inner peace. Let a peaceful thought fuel your strength in the difficult times by not allowing your circumstances to dictate your mood. Honor yourself and maintain the inner peace you deserve. It will allow you to maneuver through life's most difficult challenges with more ease and grace. Believe you are deserving of everything good.

Keep a peaceful heart and continue to engage your faith by staying positive amidst difficult times. It may mean a constant, conscious effort to reframe your thoughts, in the moment, from the negatives holding you back in order to move you forward enjoying your day. Return your thoughts to happy moments, memories, and images that give you joy, and reclaim the peace you deserve. You're worth it.

Even when troublesome events attempted to pop my powerful energy bubble of peace, joy provided an invisible shield to protect me. My spirit resisted pessimism, and peace prevailed. In spite of everything coming against me, a sense of inner peace prevailed. Victorious.

Simple (Though Not Always Easy) Steps

Stay in the moment to create the peaceful balance you need to succeed in life. This will give you the stability to move forward in a positive direction.

Create peacefulness through ME moments, meditation, and mantras. Mindfulness will create a state of peace, freeing up energy for you to pursue your passions.

Slowing down can provide a peaceful energy that will help you focus on your dreams, so you can live the life you deserve, making those dreams a reality. Don't give up! You've got this!

Enlightened Is the New Wise

It is said we become wiser with age, but wiser how? In intellect or in life's infinite experiences that provide a deeper insight to who we are and why we are here on earth? Or, perhaps, it is something even more profound. I love new opportunities to learn, grow, and expand my knowledge base to gain a better understanding of my life's purpose. But more importantly, I love the grace that enlightenment bestows upon my spirit. Enlightened is the new wise.

An open mind can receive the secret to claiming an abundant feeling of joy. With open minds, we have a sincere willingness to explore alternative possibilities, including those greater than we can currently see, and ideologies that contrast with those we consider paramount. This means we learn and grow in more profound ways when we enter each new encounter with open minds and open hearts. Open-mindedness is a more precise way to measure yourself and become fully engaged with the world you encounter. Self-discovery begins with an open awareness, which inspires peace and a joy-filled journey. Be wise and understand that enlightenment is the ability to tap into our truest self, free of fears and even sorrows.

What do you think of when you hear the word "enlightenment?" Is it a concept you feel connected with, or does it seem incredibly abstract or distant from where you are in your thoughts and contentment? Or, perhaps, it sounds like only those who devote themselves to continual self-discovery can achieve the graceful title of an "enlightened person."

I believe we all have the ability to tap into our enlightened spirit, and it doesn't have to be as profound as standing on top of a mountain in the Himalayas, softly chanting with Tibetan monks. While that does sound like an amazing experience to add to our bucket lists, we need real, achievable experiences in our everyday life to explore our enlightened, spiritual side.

Enlightenment Is Not an Enigma

Simply exploring this book and others like it brings you closer to a truly enlightened life. I love how the article "12 Necessities for an Enlightened Soul", by *Reiki Explored,* describes enlightenment. It says that an enlightened person is loving, kind, grateful, compassionate, and faithful. Those living in enlightenment genuinely care about other people, regardless of whether they care about you. They are at peace.

I imagine you can relate more closely to this than you may have imagined. Enlightenment isn't some sort of enigma or a mystical concept we can only achieve after working our whole life to understand its deepest meaning. It's much simpler than that, and I bet you now feel that *you* are in the light of enlightenment—or at least on the path towards enlightenment in your life. Staying in your own lane, lifting others, not comparing yourself to others, and releasing your fears to faith, all these empower an enlightened approach to life.

An enlightened individual doesn't need to be the center of attention to ignite their flame to glow and grow. The enlightened person thrives from a strong sense of inner peace, claiming a calm, warrior spirit. A person who lives in enlightenment has not been granted some magical power. We all have equal opportunity to connect to our enlightened spirit.

So, if you want to be more intellectual, read a book. If you want to be wiser and to seek a more enlightened life, start to let your inner light glow to transcend with a peaceful approach to loving your life. Always remember that you are the magic. You make each moment more magical simply by being true to you, and by showing up with the light of joy.

Forgiveness Perpetuates a Peaceful Spirit

Forgiveness releases past guilt and lingering feelings of resentment. In exchange, the act of forgiving yourself or someone else shapes a newfound freedom for your future. Forgiveness is like giving yourself the gift of returning back to the present moment. It's a glorious gift, granting yourself permission to start healing your heart from the hurt. Forgiveness isn't about forgetting what happened. It's all about what *you* need and has little to do with the other person. It's about reclaiming peace and contentment for your life. And you deserve nothing less.

A forgiving heart is crowned with the glory of peacefulness, forever to reign as the winner. Forgiveness gives you an opportunity to learn from the bad experience or betrayal. At the same time, you become wiser as you distance yourself from reliving the painful experience and disentangle yourself from the resentment and anger. Letting go of the grudge sets you free from feeling powerless over the situation, letting you move past the negative energy that caused the feelings of anger and bitterness in the first place. Forgiveness elevates your inner light of peacefulness.

Allow yourself the grace that only the act of forgiveness can give you. Empower your warrior spirit. Don't let one awful experience diminish your light. You've already triumphed past the adversity.

Now, hold you head high with pride, and embrace forgiveness as a true position of power and control in your life.

Forgiveness Is a Deliberate Choice

Psychologists generally define forgiveness as a "conscious, deliberate decision to release feelings of resentment or vengeance toward a person or group who has harmed you, regardless of whether they actually deserve your forgiveness." A journal from The Greater Good Science Center studies the psychology, sociology, and neuroscience of well-being. It states that, "The action of forgiving teaches skills that foster a thriving, resilient, and compassionate society, all of which are traits of a forgiving heart."

Just as important as defining forgiveness is understanding what forgiveness is *not*. Experts who study or teach forgiveness make it clear that, when you forgive, you do not gloss over or deny the seriousness of an offense against you. They also say that forgiving isn't about forgetting, nor are you disregarding the wrong-doing when you forgive someone. It goes on to describe how forgiveness doesn't require reconciliation or positive feelings towards the person you're forgiving. Instead, it's about letting go of corrosive negative feelings, letting you recognize your pain while still moving on with life.

Many psychologists also affirm that forgiveness reduces stress and anxiety, lowers cholesterol, and helps with insomnia. There are some great benefits to forgiveness. It may be difficult and seem unfair, but a tender heart strengthens with experience.

Remember that you are the only one who can decide to forgive. It's your choice. If your ego isn't letting go of a grudge, consciously put your pride aside for those who truly deserve your forgiveness, which (most definitely) includes you! You deserve forgiveness too! Forgiveness is freedom for you. Free your spirit by forgiving yourself. Forgiveness releases negative energy and keeps it from plaguing your spirit.

Yes, it's unfortunate when unfair situations come up. They happen to us all. Everyone goes through challenging circumstances. The trick is not to let life's challenges or people who've wronged you overshadow the positive moments in life. It's 110 percent your choice how long you harbor the hurt in your heart, but holding on to feelings of resentment will tarnish the good times too.

A quote, from the enlightened visionary Martin Luther King, Jr., eloquently sums up the intention of forgiveness: "We must develop and maintain the capacity to forgive. He who is devoid of the power to forgive is devoid of the power to love."

You deserve to shine, so loosen the ties of resentment and bitterness by opening your heart to forgiveness and the opportunity to experience the love you deserve. Forgiveness is a key tool to achieving best-life-ever status.

Engage with Your Emotions

Let inner peace be your secret weapon against strife. Inner peace is a powerful tool to give strength to your spirits and to bring joy to your heart, even on the darkest days. Believing that you are always deserving of inner peace will further equip you with a tool of honor. Honor yourself by not allowing your temporary circumstances to steal your inner peace. Preserving your peace of mind is not circumstantial. Inner peace should be with you each and every day, irrespective of your circumstances in that moment of time. You are equipped with this superpower of inner peace. Take hold of it and never let go.

Negative circumstances will try to take over our thoughts and steal our sense of peace, but they will fail—unless we let them succeed. Inner peace is an innate and essential tool from which to draw strength. Simply avoiding unfavorable feelings and emotions isn't a solution. We need to learn how to *process* our difficult feelings of discontentment to empower ourselves to move forward from them. Engage in your emotions!

If sorrow is what you're feeling in that very moment, validating and empathizing with your feelings is a valuable step to nurture and heal from heartache or anger or whatever it is that's coming up for you. Only when you address your emotions can you understand how to help yourself and feel closer to living a peaceful life. Validating your feelings and exploring the emotions that come up for you, in that very moment, allows you an opportunity to sort through your thoughts and identify what may be contributing to the troubles.

While not every adverse emotion that comes up can readily be linked to a direct cause-and-effect circumstance, attempting to be conscious of what causes your emotions is a step in the right direction. Sometimes we must sit still in silence to decode why we feel a certain way. At times, a bleakness may cloud our feelings, blocking any link to a straightforward explanation. There's not always an easy answer either. I am simply encouraging you to give yourself a fair opportunity to explore healing in a timely fashion, when it feels right to you. Life is too short to sit in sorrow. So, give yourself the identical grace to heal as you did to hurt.

Mend with love, using positive affirmations and an "always believe in yourself" attitude to heal your heart. I don't want you to waste a minute stirring up feelings of sorrow by reflecting on past moments, holding on to regret, or dwelling in anger. Living day-in and day-out with these emotions unmistakably carries little value in terms of boosting your inner spirit, while disengaging will definitely raise your inner peace to foster joy.

Recognizing who we can and cannot trust with our feelings is important to maintaining our personal peace. Even with the best intentions, it can be challenging to say the right thing when someone is going through difficulties. When people mean to be helpful, they can unintentionally put their foot in their mouth and say something that makes you feel worse. Sometimes we just need someone to listen. Make a shortlist of people in your life who will offer you a sincere ear—people who will be understanding and will truly care for and support you. Reach out to someone you trust.

Live an empowered life by taking a proactive approach to inspire yourself. Your words have tremendous strength and therefore you need to choose them wisely. Build a foundation of peace and positivity through your own words, since we are the product of what we say to ourselves. Say something amazing!

Tips and Tools to Preserve Your Peace

Protecting Your Peace

This will help you maneuver more fluently through life's most unchartered terrain with a graceful glow. Grace gives you the freedom to make mistakes along the way. *A peaceful heart survives the storm.*

This means you must constantly be conscious, in the moment, to reframe negative thoughts that hold you back from enjoying the day.

Honor Yourself

Maintain the inner peace you deserve by refusing to allow external circumstances to dictate how you feel. The unfair situation has already taken too much as it is!

Let Go of the Limiting Belief

A limiting belief is an unfounded assumption that you can't achieve your intended goals (E.g., "I don't deserve to be happy.") but having nothing to support that thought. Limiting beliefs can most definitely hold you back in life. Set yourself free from them.

The Power of Positivity

Similar to the translucent glow of light, positivity emerges from our spirit to miraculously radiate joy out to the world. Switching on a light of positivity adds a shine of possibility. Give yourself and others positive encouragement to inspire a brighter day for everyone. Sometimes, all it takes is a quick burst of positivity to brighten an otherwise gloomy day. Negative feelings of gloom and despair readily cast clouds over our life, leaving little room for us to see the light of joy. Refocus on a positive outlook as a way to switch a light on the situation. Positivity always brings possibility. Negativity never knows what's best, because it's always focused on the worst!

No one actually likes living in the shadows of negativity. However, at times, we can grow accustomed to and even comfortable in the darkness of disparity. Familiarity seems like the safest option, despite the dreary disfunction the darkness brings along with it. Weary people claim caution as their course of action, while looming in the shelter of life's shadows. They even begin to fear the light that positivity beams into the world. Wounded from life's trials, they become too comfortable in the disaster zone of darkness to dare take a peek at the world with positivity or a perspective of possibility. Quick to point blame at the world for their hardships, negativity takes over their lives. They lose sight of the fact that positivity is entirely their choice. Switching the signal to a positive frequency is in their hands, and more importantly, their mindset. Our thoughts dictate how we show up in life, and they can be a clear predictor of our direction, whether it be positive or negative.

A miraculous, magical glow warms our hearts when positivity is present.

Positivity is a paramount coping mechanism that cultivates a feeling of joy. Anything is possible with positivity. Positivity will propel you to catapult over the problem without losing your joy—even in the most difficult times. Positivity is a boost that drives your energy towards a solution.

Purposeful Positivity

Be positive on purpose. Let positivity be purposeful in all you do. Take action in your own life to send a positive vibe into the world. A positive attitude is a daily action that needs to be intentional. Begin the moment you wake up in the morning, with positive affirmations, streamlining your thoughts to create a positive outlook for the day. Monitor your thoughts to identify when your mind starts to shift from focusing on the positive to emphasizing the negative.

The moment you identify your thoughts as negative, reframe them back to a positive. Your attitude is a choice—one you make every day. As per the law of attraction, you attract what you focus on. If it's positive, you will attract positive things in your life. If it's negative, then you will attract negative things in your life. You will make a wise decision by knowing that you need to let go of thoughts and actions that don't serve you in a positive way.

Just like a negative person's energy can bring you down, positive encouragement can lift others up. Negative people distract you from feeling good about yourself, distancing you from your dreams. You're simply too important to let negativity stall you from your destiny. Focus your thoughts on all the positive possibilities for your life, regardless of what or who confronts you during the day. One way I action a positive presents is by always equipping myself with a smile.

My smile is my *superpower*—shining brightly out into the world as a shield of protection. If I'm nervous or anxious entering a room filled with new people, I always take along my trusty smile; it never fails to lead me directly to the kindhearted. I instantly recognize them as they are smiling right back at me.

Smiling is a universal sign of friendship—generally returned by those who understand the powerful message a smile radiates in any situation.

Believe me when I say that it's pretty hard to cry when you're beaming from ear to ear. My smile is my secret weapon against anyone who tries to bring down my positive vibe. Go ahead, road-ragers: *Honk,* because I didn't accelerate through the amber light for you to run a red. A picture perfect smile and enthusiastic wave will be my response. No one is *stealing* my sunshine.

Positivity is priceless. So, positively *don't* give other peeps the power to *steal* your shimmering light. Positivity is way too valuable and so are you! Surround yourself with positive people who lift your internal light.

Eradicating the Patterns of Negative Thoughts

Negative self-talk includes phrases like this: *You are not good enough. You do not measure up. You are a failure. You are not based on truth.* These negative thoughts are manifested by fear. They are driven by fear, not truth. So, when fear-based, self-defeating thoughts creep in, you need to combat them by reframing your thoughts to positive affirmations about yourself. Replace limiting beliefs by claiming ownership of positivity: *I am deserving of good things! I am awesome! I am capable! I am lovable! I am filled with joy!* Declare positivity to rain positive possibilities over your life.

Nagging, negative thoughts can stem from a problem that is not visibly present on the surface, often called the *root problem.* Such negative patterns of thought are ingrained in us from childhood. We can be so conditioned into negativity that positive thinking just seems unnatural. It becomes part of our brain's programming. These problems are not easy to overcome, because no matter how much you throw in positivity from the top, if the root is shaky, it will keep throwing that positivity out the window. You must identify what those patterns are, why are they there, and how to eradicate them. Only then will a permanent solution pop up to address this issue.

Eradicate the patterns of negative thoughts by exploring what caused you to dip into despair. Resurface the reality of the issue to uproot what's gripping you in negativity. Actively identify the core of your negative thoughts to recognize their root cause. Knowing what is triggering a negative cloud over your thoughts will help eliminate its effects. Once you have that awareness, you can then make a conscious choice to shift that mindset and choose a perspective that is not self-sabotaging.

Viewing your life through a negative lens means you see only a narrow scope of life's possibilities. It's like seeing only half a picture and being asked to draw the whole image. It's not fair. You've only got half the view of what it could look like. It's the same thing when someone focuses only on the negative side. Only half of the ideas are seen, without any light given to the whole picture and the full range of possibilities that are truthfully there.

Start rewriting your personal narrative. Explore multiple pathways to experience life, especially in challenging seasons. Step out of the shadows and focus your thoughts on nurturing a peaceful presence in your life. An optimistic view of the day will help you combat any trouble that comes your way. You are truly a gift to this world and positively deserve to be celebrated. Start the celebration by positively boosting your day with positivity.

Positivity releases a joyful energy within your own heart to sail strong against any storm or season in your life. Don't let negativity sink you deep below the surface. Let positivity renew the wind beneath your inner sails, and free you to start popping up each day with positivity.

Tips and Tools to Let Go of a Negative Mindset

If you focus your thoughts only on the positive aspects of life, and how those positive aspects give you a better standing than many others, your brain will start rewiring around positive ideas. Opening the doorway to possibility is positively game changing!

By encouraging the power of joy, I'm purposefully hoping to reboot positivity in your life, even in times of tremendous difficulties. Use this book as a guide for keeping peace in your heart and a smile on your face. Take its words as encouragement to recalibrate your thoughts from negative to positive. Then you will not have surrendered that time as a casualty. You are a warrior of peace and joy.

Validate your feelings. There's a reason for the emotions you're experiencing. Ask what steps will move you towards feeling more content. Stay determined to try different ways to encourage yourself. Remind yourself to stay positive, and reframe to a positive thought when a negative one pops into your mind. Positivity will help conquer each obstacle with joy, and you will become victorious in your journey with positivity. Joy is different for everyone, but the one constant is the boost of joy you receive from keeping a positive mindset.

Chapter Seven
Meditation and Mantras

"When you sit in meditation, feel the joy in
your soul."
Ma Jaya

You might be seasoned at meditating, or simply reading through this chapter with an open mind to explore how meditation can help increase your joy factor in life. Either way, know that meditation can easily be summed up in two words: quiet time. This is as simple as it gets—straight to the point, and 110 percent accurate! Meditating doesn't need to be more complex than this simple statement. It's just a moment of quiet time focused on our thoughts.

When I was in my early twenties, meditation re-emerged as a "new trend" and I was as trendy as they got! I didn't like missing out on anything popular, so if *Cosmo* magazine suggested it as a must-do in one of their coolest-ever quizzes, I was in! Inner enlightenment, here I come! But between you and me, I didn't get exactly what I was supposed to be doing. Leave it to me to complicate the easiest inner source of self-comfort and discovery. I'd sit in silence the whole time, wondering if this was it, and asking myself what I was missing. I concluded that I needed more information on how this meditation thing really worked. So, after signing out several books from the public library on how to master meditation like the experts, I came to the profound realization that meditation was as simple as *quiet time.* Apparently I'd way overcomplicated (something I did a lot back then) this easy process of simply taking time to reflect and connect with your thoughts. What I was really missing was the point! This was a mind-blowing revelation for my younger self, which also taught me a valuable lesson in not overthinking things. Ever since, I've adored meditating and mindfulness as a calming tool to add clarity to my life.

Meditation and mantras are the processes of mindfulness that calms your mind and redirects your thoughts to rest on something positive. Meditation is a magical tool to shift your thoughts and move your energy in a positive direction. Pause and take a meaningful minute to intentionally shift your energy away from what's bringing you down. Move towards lifting thoughts of self-love. Whether it's your very first try or we call you guru or you're anywhere in between, remember: It can be as easy as *quiet time.* Focus your thoughts on gratitude, love, positivity, harmony, or my personal favorite, joy! If it calms you, then it's working. Just take it one bold breath at a time.

It's less important what you ponder than the feelings and emotions you generate through the process of mindfulness. Heck, from time to time, I've been known to meditate on cookies! As a self-proclaimed Cookie Monster, why wouldn't I focus on cookies, considering how happy I feel when I'm eating them? Why not! The kids and I have a favorite bakery back in Arkansas called Bizzy B's Bakery. We'd love grabbing a cookie on a warm, sunny day, which it often was in Arkansas, and stopping by our favorite park to enjoy them! When I am feeling homesick for that place, I take a quick moment to reflect on all those delicious, delectable cookies, and that brings me a joyful moment. I say you should use whatever thought clears the air of despair. If it works to calm your mind or slow your heart from racing, then it's a winner.

Of course, following classic methods of meditation are always an awesome option, too. Follow your intuition. I actively practice several different approaches depending on the moment, how I am feeling, and what emotions are coming up for me. All methods should be taken into consideration. Some of the ways might be as simple as taking a quick moment before leaving my car before a big meeting or a coaching session with a new client. I'll sit in silence with my eyes closed in a moment of gratitude, centering myself back to what's truly important in my life.

Or, if I have more time, I will stand quietly with my eyes closed, facing the direction of the sun and absorbing the pure sounds of nature. You likely have some favorite meditation methods too, or might be open to trying some new ones.

Meditation Advantages

One of the most beneficial treatments Jeffery and I explored while faithfully, patiently, persistently seeking healing for Jeffery was meditation. Jeffery discovered it was an amazing activity for his mind, body, and soul connection. For him, it acted as key distraction at a time when he felt little control over his life as he healed. We were fortunate enough that one of Jeffery's employers initiated a few sessions with a "meditation guru" who came right to the house. He taught Jeffery the fundamentals of meditation. Though no closer to a cure for Jeffery's traumatic brain injury, meditation definitely solidified Jefferys feelings, giving him a new technique to distract himself from the constant clutches of pain and symptoms.

I came across some interesting facts on meditation in an article by Lachlan Brown from *Hack Spirit*, with statistics supporting just some of the many advantages of meditation.

- Today, the number of people who meditate globally is estimated to be anywhere between two-hundred and five-hundred million.

- In American, 40 percent of adults claim to meditate at least once a week.
- Since 2012, the number of children who've tried meditation has grown ten times.
- From those surveyed, 75 percent of insomniacs who've started a daily meditation plan are able to fall asleep within twenty minutes of going to bed.
- Practicing meditation for six to nine months may reduce anxiety by 60 percent.

There are many types of meditation, but however you label "meditating," it's essentially about the essence of your thoughts. Meditating allows you a brief opportunity to truly connect with all your senses and to explore how you feel without external influences or distractions.

No Wrong Way to Meditate

Meditation is as easy as finding a quiet space and moment where you can feel comfortable, breathe freely, and close your eyes. Then, you release past regrets and let go of guilt. Focus your thoughts on what brings you joy, contemplate gratitude, and focus your mind on a solution to eliminate a problem in your life. Or, perhaps manifest a dream to come true by chanting about it quietly between each breath. Meditating should feel freeing. It's supposed to be cleansing. I believe taking time to meditate is a beautiful expression of self-love. There really is no wrong way to meditate. It's about honoring your inner voice by investing in small pockets of time throughout your busy life to listen to how you're feeling.

For me, meditating streamlines my emotions back to a place of peace, helping me own my feelings and direct my thoughts for more clarity moving forward. It's a mindful time, reflecting on my thoughts, directing my energy to seek a solution to situations that might be causing me stress. Or I meditate simply as a source of joy, manifesting new ideas and directions that will further enhance opportunities to live my best life ever.

The Vibrations of Mantras

Mantras are repetitive sounds used to penetrate the depths of the unconscious mind, and adjust the vibration of all aspects of your being. Mantras are vibrated through chanting aloud, mental practice, or by listening to them. The experience of how sound vibrations affect your being is called Naad yoga. Use it by singing mantras in the mornings or on your way to work. Sing mantras out loud or sing them to yourself.

You may know the Muppets, the zany group of puppets created by the late Jim Henson, who live on through a carefully preserved legacy that brings us decades of infectious-fun for the whole family. One of the Muppet-inspired songs—or should I say, sounds—is, "Mahna mahna!" It's an extra fun mantra that contours amazing memories of watching *The Muppet Show* as a family when I was growing up. And now, my own family enjoys sharing in the fun and joy that those energetic, zany, fun-loving Muppets always give us! Yes, of course, "Mahna mahna" can most definitely be a mantra! It's okay to make mantras fun. The intent to center your thoughts can be done in any way that you're comfortable with.

For about a year, I would wake up in the morning, and as I was getting ready, I'd mantra *The Lego Movie* song "Everything is AWESOME!!! The lyrics remind us that everything is cool when you're a part of a team! I owe that upbeat chant so much praise for giving me a positive vibe each morning. It was literally impossible not to feel happy chanting those energizing words of encouragement. It made me smile, feel gratitude for my family, and start my day with the energy of joy. Of course, more traditional mantras are beneficial in many ways. I have enjoyed many moments practicing chants, as well. I just want you to feel comfortable experimenting with different approaches to mantras.

More About ME Moments!

Meditation is an act to calm you mind, spirit, and soul. Take a moment to meditate on something that fuels joy inside your heart. Now, imagine how incredible you would feel if you could keep thoughts of joy in your heart at all times, I believe you can. That's the power of joy.

Throughout Jeffery's twenty-seven-month traumatic brain injury recovery, I began devoting quick moments of time throughout the day to practicing *ME (my energy) moments*. These ME moments held space for self-love. They were tiny pockets of time just for me to focus solely on my personal energy. ME moments reclaimed valuable energy back into my spirit. I felt myself regaining a sense of control. I felt more confident and recharged, like I was placing myself in control of my current situation. It could be as quick as a few second or as long as I had to drink a cup of tea in the early morning hours before life's reluctant scope would try to dull the day. ME moments let the light back into my vision and allowed me to see the potential, not just the problem. Making a conscious decision to slow down for a few seconds in the day had a huge impact on how I was feeling throughout the day. Simple ME moments gave me joy to boost my day.

A fast-paced lifestyle manifests many external stresses that can distract us from what holds true meaning to us. I like to take hold of my thoughts with a ME moment. I shift my energy back to "the me I want to be" mode, which helps develop a stronger love and awareness for myself and makes me understand who I am and what I truly want. You can use ME moments the same way. Streamline your thoughts back to happy moments, memories, and images that give you the most joy.

So, whether you end with a *namaste* or a *mahna mahna,* it should be true to who you are and how you roll in life. I want you to roll freely, feeling much love and joy. Meditation is one tool to get you there!

Start Mindful Exercises

Exercise releases serotonin in your body, improving your mood and increasing your happiness levels. Engaging in mindful exercise is a brilliant way to take care of your body *and* mind. Below are some examples of mindfulness.

Present Moment Mindset

Focus your thoughts on doing *one thing* in this very moment.

Self-Acceptance

Accept yourself as you are in this very moment, and feel proud.

A Holistic Approach to Self-Love

Be grateful for each individual part of your life. You will beam brighter when all aspects of yourself come together, providing a harmonious balance between your mind, body, and soul.

Breathing

Use breathing as a tool to refuel your spirit. Taking a deep breath allows you a moment to restore a peaceful feeling in your spirit. There are multiple benefits of breathing. Caregivers will have a reduced chance of burnouts. The usual body reaction to fatigue and stress will be better regulated. Chronic pain will be better managed, depression and diabetic symptoms will be reduced. Blood pressure, heart rate, and stress levels will be lowered. Breathing is a great thing!

Breathing Techniques

Here are few different breathing techniques that you can follow.

Yoga Breathing

The most common breathing technique is yoga breathing, where you slowly draw your breath in, and pause, then slowly exhale, letting all your breath out, and then pause again. This process is repeated to calm stress.

Abdominal Breathing

This is one of my favorites. Abdominal breathing is for beginners when they start to meditate. It is practiced by placing one hand on your stomach while placing the other one on chest. Then you take a deep breath from the nose. You can feel your hand on your stomach move as it inflates the diaphragm with air. Then you slowly release your breath.

Alternate Nostril Breathing

This one's fun and very beneficial for reviving energy. You plug your left nostril with your left thumb, and breathe through your right nostril. Then you remove the thumb and repeat the procedure for right nostril. You repeat this until your body is reenergized.

And last but not least, my personal breathing technique:

Blowing-out the Butterflies

Take a deep breath all the way in through your nose until you can't take in any more air. Then slowly exhale the entire breath to release the metaphoric butterflies that represent your anxieties and stresses. The butterflies fly higher that your worries, so the butterflies will carry your worries away. All the while, you're releasing negative energies from your heart and extinguishing fear with every breath. Practice this breathing technique to flutter and soar as the majestic movements of a beautiful butterfly—transform forward more freely.

These are a few of the breathing techniques that help reduce butterflies, anxiety, and stress. Think of breathing as refueling your spirit, so it can soar higher simply by taking some meaningful breaths. So, boldly breathe your way toward your best life ever.

As Simple as Spaghetti

Take a ME moment to breathe and meditate on a joyful memory. Move forward with joy and in peace. You deserve to give yourself a moment of peace. Allow these joyful moments to settle in your heart, by refueling your spirit with joy.

It's as simple as spaghetti. When you feel like you're reaching the point of boiling over like a pot of spaghetti, disengage the intensity of the flame, and stop a moment to reclaim your cool. Take a moment to redirect your energy when you feel like your thoughts are boiling over. Reaching a boiling point could have developed over the course of the day or been brewing for much longer. A series of small stresses can create chaos little by little, until finally something puts you at a personal boiling point, or it could be that one super-sized situation that has suddenly triggered stress to surface all at once. A ME moment will recharge and refocus your energy back to a positive mindset. ME moments are like pressing a reset button to strengthen your spirit and bring joy back in the moment.

ME moments can be taken at any moment of the day, anywhere. Take a quiet space in your thoughts and draw a beautiful breath to create joy. Listen to the rhythm of your breathing. Meditate and tell yourself that you are deserving of this ME moment—a quick moment just for you to determine what you need by tapping into your intuition. Listen to your internal dialogue. ME moments help increase clarity and decrease stress that can otherwise lead us to feel anxious. ME moments release guilt and judgment, so you can build on a foundation of self-acceptance by resurfacing the energy of joy back into your life. Accept that you truly deserve a constant stream of joy energizing your life. Our thoughts control our direction, so direct yourself to move forward with the things that make you happy and bring you the most joy! ME moments are a little gift to your spirit.

"*It's for You*"

Chapter Eight
Hello, It's Your Intuition Calling

*"Have the courage to follow your heart and intuition.
They somehow already know what you truly want to
become. Everything else is secondary."*
– Steve Jobs

Our intuition is our inner voice giving a gentle nudge or sometimes screaming *stop!* It's a strong suggestion in the pit of your stomach pleading with you to move in a particular direction. Yet, you only acknowledge it passively, and continue throughout the day, only to discover later that this hunch was right, and you just missed out on an amazing opportunity. Sound familiar to anyone else? It's definitely happened many times to me, especially in my younger years before I began exploring the fascinating, mystical power of my intuition.

Hopefully, you're acting on your intuition and reaping the powerful rewards that come with following it! I imagine almost all of us have experienced a situation where our gut was telling us one thing and our logical mind worked diligently to override our intuition's awesome intent to empower us to become victorious. Just like a true and loyal friend, our intuition doesn't take it personally, and reacts with the same determination and insight the next time it eagerly tries its darnedest to inspire us to take the very best path for our life.

Our intuition is an inner feeling persuading you towards one direction over another. Intuition emerges from our unconscious thoughts alerting us with subtle signs after it notices something isn't right or that someone isn't being as transparent as they seem. Our intuition picks up on those unsettling vibes and tries its best to steer us from harm's way. Yet, our intuition is only as good as our ability to apply its direction to our everyday life.

Intuition in Action

A sign from your intuition could be as simple as the desire to call a friend when they pop up in your mind. You could discover in that call that they hesitated to reach out but really needed your encouragement, and this ended up being the perfect timing to lift their day. Your intuition called it, by calling on you to call your friend.

Intuition can be as easy as understanding when you need a break or extra rest. Acting on these inner nudges is one way to honor your intuition. In this example, simply take time to care for yourself. Thank you for the reminder, my intuitive self!

Your intuition is there to support you, sort of like a service announcement. It's like the rapid weather alert warning at the bottom of the screen when you're watching your local news station. That's a message you don't want to take lightly—especially true in Arkansas when tornado season hits. Those storms popped up out of nowhere. One night when my kids where little, I looked out the window at the back of our home to see a beautiful, clear, sunset sky over the golf course. Twenty minutes later, after cuddling and tucking in my three little amigos, it looked like the opening scene from *The Wizard of Oz* outside. The sky had darkened and the trees were whipping around in what seemed to be over ninety-miles-per-hour winds. Stuff was flying past the window and the neighborhood storm sirens started to sound in the distance. Jeffery and I carried all three kids down two levels of stairs and into the back of the basement—our designated storm area—in record time. Sometimes, my intuition told me a storm was coming, we'd avoid this desperate move by having the kids sleep in the basement every night for a week. Ah, the good old days! But just like the weather forecast's warning, intuition acts as a source of information alerting you to what's in your best interests.

Everyone can tap into their intuitiveness to make everyday decisions. Sometimes, the signs aren't so subtle. Your subconscious may send you a flaming red flag when things don't feel right. That's your subconscious thoughts trying to catch your attention, so take care to listen up! I tend to listen in often, especially when I am feeling uneasy about a person or situation. I will sit in meditation as a way to calm my senses. Calming my senses seems to make space for my intuition to give a clear response to a pending decision.

I believe my intuition is God's gentle nudge in the right direction. I continuously tap into my intuition, for it always proves to be right. I'm extremely grateful for this inner guidance, and I take full advantage of the knowledge it provides me. Even now, when I'm not in a challenging season like during Jeffery's recovery, I take plenty of time to listen to my intuitive energy pointing me in the right direction.

Intuition is like driving on cruise control. You are in the moment, and everything is set to keep you moving forward with little to no thought or effort. When you get an instant feeling of good or bad, it is your intuition nudging you towards your next best move. All of us have felt it before. It's an internal urge to move in one direction for no apparent reason. You follow suit, and everything works out in such an amazing way that you have to pause and look back to see how it all connected and materialized. That's your intuition at work.

Driven by Intuition

My becoming a certified life coach was driven entirely by my intuition. We were eight months into Jeffery's traumatic brain injury recovery when his health suddenly spiraled downhill, and he ended up recovering in the hospital. It was in this time that I started pursuing the idea of going back to work. I had been away from the workforce as a full-time mom raising our three beautiful kids, and never had any real plans of returning. Our family grew fast, as we had Savannah, Sienna, and Liam all within three years and four months.

I loved my job as Super Mom Extraordinaire and our family was blessed to be able to have me stay home. I felt so very blessed to be a mother and loved, loved, loved participating in activities to support my kids. I was a homeroom mom for two of their classes simultaneously(I would have done all classes if the school had let me, and I cheered them on in tennis, dance, golf, soccer, Taekwondo, and numerous other activities. For me, it was heavenly; however, given our circumstances, I felt it would be wise to start exploring other future directions.

As you may have guessed, I fueled my pursuit with faith, as I do in most situations. I prayed on what I could do as a career that would still allow me to be actively involved in my children's lives. A new career needed to be in line with my values. So, I prayed with gratitude—grateful that God had an abundance of opportunities for me. I boldly asked him to send a significant sign for the direction I should explore. I always believe in being bold and direct, and that indecisiveness is an extravagant misuse of precious time and energy. Now, please believe me when I say that, within twenty-four hours, someone randomly mentioned that given my ability to keep a joyful attitude during trying times, I would be an amazing life coach. This person had no idea about my prayers or even that I was at a crossroads, contemplating a new career. God is good.

Wow! I had never dreamed about becoming a professional life coach, yet it immediately struck a chord within my spirit, seeming like an awesome idea—an intuitive surge fueled by faith! That being said, I wasn't exactly sure what a life coach was. Still, I was more than joyed to do a little research to find out. It was even more incredible that the strangely-timed advice fueled immense feelings of joy, peace, excitement, and contentment, which invaded my senses all at once. It felt like my passions were popping! I intuitively knew, without question, that this was the answer to my prayer.

It was only a short time after that experience that I declared in my mind and to my heart that I would also write a book to encourage others to connect with joy throughout all life circumstances. This was a bold claim for someone who's never written more than a few pages for essays at university. But (as I say with a humble heart and much gratitude) I guess following my gut on this one really materialized! Yay for me for listening! And big mental hugs to you for being part of my journey with joy! I spent every extra minute for many, many, many months writing this very book—the one that I dreamed of and declared about amidst such a challenging season. I still become teary eyed every time I realize that I did just that. Now, my passions are popping with joy and pride. Be bold with your dreams, because you're most definitely worth it! Follow that inner voice to discover how to make all your dreams come true! I sincerely want that for you.

I owe my intuition much gratitude, for it is a key light that guides my journey. I can always depend on it, simply by taking a moment to listen to my inner voice. It always seems to lead me in the direction to shine brighter. Listen in to your own inner voice and discover your shine too.

The Tug-of-War

At times, your mind and heart play a tug-of-war of sorts. Your thoughts and emotions leave you unsure of the right choice. Often, you are tired and unable to make the best decision for yourself. There is an internal struggle. On one side, your brain is telling you to move forward with sound logic. On the other side, your heart is moving in a completely different direction. Let your intuition settle the dispute.

Sometimes, we overthink a situation and move too quickly with no thought, racing ahead with feelings from the heart instead of logic. Our intuition guides us in the best direction. Don't get distracted from your feelings. Our thoughts often shift us away from simply living in the moment. Let your intuitive energy deepen your connection to living in the present moment, while strengthening the power of joy to surge in your life.

There are pros and cons to everything in life, and the unfavorable side to intuitiveness shows up when we don't tap into its energy. Not taking advantage of that gentle nudge from our intuition can gravely affect a situation. At one time or another, we've all heard words like, "Darn, I wish I would have listened to my gut," or, "I wish I'd have followed how I truly felt inside." Sometimes, our intuition doesn't send the same message as our brain. Intuition is not based on logic or conscious thinking. It's an inner thought or feeling pulling you in the right direction. It's innate, and it's in all of us. We all have the ability to tap into it, yet we don't all use this ability to our full advantage.

Tapping into Your Intuition

Our core values seem to rise within as we give attention to our intuition. This should be reassuring for anyone still on the sidelines, and not so intuitively savvy-minded—yet! Jump up and connect with your intuition simply by recognizing it as an inner resource available to you at any given moment. Practice patience to encourage intuitive energy to empower and guide your journey. Also, practice makes perfect.

Take ME moments to listen to and hear what your intuition is telling you. Don't allow outside chatter to distract you from following your gut feelings. Others may try to sway your thoughts or influence you by tugging at your heart strings. Draw a metaphoric line in the sand to separate yourself from their idling distractions, then silently lend an ear to your heart's soothing and persuasive voice gently pushing you towards the most advantageous path. Explore the direction your intuition is pushing you towards. I believe it's guiding you towards success, while granting you an opportunity to feel joy, knowing you're moving towards living your best life ever—the life God intended for you, the life you most deeply deserve.

In recent years, intuition has remained a hot topic amongst psychologists. Researchers have found a way to measure this feeling of intuition and conducted a number of experiments on how "nonconscious emotional information" from the brain impacts decision making. In one experiment, participants were asked to figure out if the white-colored dots appearing on the screen in front of them were moving right or left. During that process, participants were shown subliminal images to activate their intuitive response. Interestingly, the researchers found out that, when participants experienced a positive subliminal image, they were able to make accurate interpretations. This means that intuition and our subconscious mind plays a huge role in making powerful decisions in life.

I'll leave it up to you—or should I say, up to your intuition—to decide whether you should listen when your inner voice is trying desperately to catch you on speed dial. I know life is busy, and we don't always feel like we have the time to listen to our inner voice. But I know how much it's helped me over the years, and I want you to enjoy the same benefits, with the answers coming from a pretty awesome source: yourself! It's worth taking the time to listen. I consider my intuition a gift of grace. It's a loyal mentor who most definitely has my best interests at heart.

The author, inspirational speaker, and independent film-maker Carol Chapman has a quote that made me smile. She said, "One great advantage of intuitive decision making: You can know much more through your intuition than you can through making decisions through logic or emotion. One great disadvantage of intuitive decision making: You have to follow it." That's fun food for thought! See what your gut is telling you before you make any decision.

Chapter Nine
Run Your Own Race

"Comparison is the thief of joy."
– Theodore Roosevelt

We can learn a valuable lesson from the story of the tortoise and the hare, an age-old tale that offers us wisdom about running our own race and pacing ourselves along life's journey. In the classic tale, the eighteenth-century author Aesop tells of a race between a fast but often-distracted hare and a slow but relentless tortoise.

The Tortoise and the Hare

There is a swift hare who relentlessly taunts a slow-moving tortoise. The tortoise becomes irritated with the hare's overbearing behavior and constant teasing, so he decides to challenge the hare to a race. The hare, of course, eagerly accepts the challenge, never once considering that the tortoise could win.

In an instant, the hare leaves the tortoise far behind in his dust. This leaves the hare more confident and self-assured than ever, and he believes he will win with ease. So, midway through the race, the smug hare decides to take a nap, although unfortunately for him, he naps for too long. All the while, the determined tortoise keeps a steady pace and wins the race with a cunning, persistent pace.

The tortoise eventually defeating the hare coined the term, "slow and steady wins the race." The moral of the story is that you can still be successful by doing things slowly and steadily, and that acting hastily can actually slow you down from seeing success.

The hare is defeated because he did not value his innate ability to be faster than the tortoise. He let his smug attitude distract him from achieving his full potential, demonstrating how a poor attitude stood in the way of success.

It is said that, "The tortoise is a symbol of wisdom and knowledge, and is able to defend himself on his own. Creation is associated with the tortoise, and it is also believed that the tortoise bears the burden of the whole world." Both the story and the saying are beautiful lessons in learning the value of pacing yourself to achieve success.

They teach us not to judge a book by its cover. Look what happened to the hare after his quick judgement of the tortoise. He paid a grave price for his generalization and thoughtlessness via a big serving of *humble pie*. It reminds us to be open minded and stay determined. It tells us not to quit, nor worry about everyone else's pace, but to focus on developing our own groove and the perfect pace to win at our own race. It tells us to release feelings of comparison, because we don't have time to waste "caring about the hare," so to speak. The hares we encounter in life move way too fast to recognize what they might be missing out on until it's too late.

Above all, the story tells us it's about the *journey* and the strides you make along the way. Journey with joy!

It's About You

Run your own race. Do not waste precious time and energy comparing yourself to what other people are doing. Counting other peoples' steps will surely distract you from advancing your own strides towards achieving success in life. If you permit your thoughts to dwell on other peoples' achievements, you will actually slow down your personal growth. Your own success will become stagnant, while you become further distanced from accomplishing your dreams.

Believing in yourself is truly the most powerful tool to inspire success. You must first believe it to see it! A simple way to drive your dreams forward is by simply believing in yourself, standing strong with your sights set on victory, and envisioning your very own success story. Design your dream, and envision success. Start today.

Staying focused on your own race is important for living your best life ever. Take small steps throughout your day to refocus your energy towards what drives you forward. You possess the greatest vested interest in your own success. So, invest the time and energy in self-development. Don't let anything or anyone keep you from accomplishing your goals. You are the only one who can drive your dreams forward. Go claim success as your story!

Write Your Own Success Story

Run your own race by establishing an alliance with yourself—an alliance between your mind and spirit to inspire your inner warrior to thrive. Simply aiming your attention in the direction of your personal goals, and what brings you the most joy in life, is a fabulous first step. Then recognize that you and you alone can stir up success. Become your own advocate by believing in yourself. Be confident, stay determined, work smart, and never give up.

Refuse failure by recognizing that each failed attempt is merely a stepping stone towards success. Consider failure as a new opportunity to try again with a more enlightened approach. Try again using what you've learned and how you've grown from each past experience. Sometimes, we learn and grow more from the failed attempts than from our successes. Don't drag failure forward by holding tightly to self-defeating thoughts. Stop stewing in sorrow over previous disappointments. Life is a continuum of cliffhangers, so quickly turn the page and set your sights towards the next chapter in your life. Step forward with the intent to succeed. Be the hero in your story. An unwritten ending never sees what truly could have been, only a game of should've, would've, could've, and much regret.

Life should excite you in the same way that reading a tantalizing tale or a mystifying mystery novel does, inspiring an intrigue that won't let you stop reading. Imagine living with an inner excitement to discover what will happen next, leaving you giddy with anticipation. What awesome adventure will happen next? Inspire for yourself the same enthusiasm within your own narrative. Envision your personal biography as a success story.

Do not let one failed situation define your future. Wipe the slate clean of mistakes, and declare success over each area of your life. Declare a new standard by not settling into failure. Rise up and greet success, for failure is not your final story. You have amazing accomplishments in your future. Make your life a story of the ages.

You Are Deserving of Greatness

Push past the parameters of a fear-to-fail mindset. Stop focusing on staying stuck in failure, and stop telling yourself that you will never get beyond this one failed attempt. Or even *many* failed attempts. It's absolutely not true. You can succeed, and you will. You must reboot and repair your pride to advance your inner greatness. Greatness is in you.

Believe you are deserving of greatness. This needs to become your reframed focus on gathering greatness in life. And greatness is what you deserve. Fretting over failure is a frightening way to miss out on your own destiny, so reframe your thoughts to move forward from failure. Interpreting past failures as merely part of the process to succeed will inevitably open up new avenues towards success.

Failure is Not Fatal

Failure is not fatal to your future. If you are breathing, then you most definitely have been granted a new opportunity to succeed. It is imperative to angle each failed situation away from your heart, so you don't assume the role of a victim. Feeling frustrated, disappointed, or like you are incompetent are all natural reactions to any fall in life. And, although the situation may seem like a setback, injuring your ego or bruising your confidence, failure is most certainly not fatal to your future.

So, please, set your pride aside. Do not stand in your own way of success with the limiting belief that your story is over just because you didn't succeed on your first or even your eleventh try. Your failed attempts are not the ending. The failure you experienced is actually setting you up with greater knowledge, so you can rise higher and expand on the greatness within you.

Instead of idling in despair, begin to reroute your goals by learning to recognize the value each challenge provides along the way. Embrace a failed attempt at success simply as a misstep. Then reroute back towards the path to success. Letting go of past failures often leads us to accelerate towards accomplishing our goals faster than we first anticipated—even if we don't realize the benefits of the misstep at the time. Don't let failing slow you down. Hold a resilient stance. Resurrect your dreams with determination, and direct your steps back on track to victory.

The only way failing becomes fatal is if you don't get back up again after an unsuccessful attempt. Our perception of failure sets the pace for future success. When we accept failure as part of the process of success, we don't waste precious energy and time being discouraged. We simply try again, always staying committed, not giving up or feeling inadequate. We recognize failure is part of the process of becoming successful. We all deserve the grace to retake steps on our journey. So, continue to redirect your vision, even when it takes real courage.

One of my favorite quotes is, "When one door closes, open it back up. It's a door. That's how they work!" The author is unknown, but the sentiment is true. Don't let disappointments lock you out of the possibility of achieving your dreams. Trying again turns the key closer to unlocking success.

Don't You Dare Compare

Comparing yourself, your story, or experiences to those of others is simply counterproductive. It's like comparing apples to watermelons. It's just not a logical measure of comparison. Instead, counter feelings of comparison and jealousy that may overwhelm your thoughts by reframing them. Take a positive outlook of self-advocacy and determination. Redirect your light back to the path of success, knowing you deserve nothing less than the best on your journey. Distractions are detours that slow down success. Maintain your momentum with the power of joy.

We've all met people who thrive on conflict and competition, and inevitably situations may arise where those people will try to provoke you to compete. An invitation to participate can happen in any situation. Believe it or not, I've even encountered a pop-up challenge while shopping. A complete stranger at the grocery store tried their hardest to race me down the aisle. It was apparent they had a need for speed, but I simply slowed down and smiled, which seemingly infuriated them, as they scowled and raced by me even faster. The first, bold step to winning at your own race is to realize that someone who tries to provoke competition might not even recognize that they're driven by their own egotistical games. You have zero obligation to take part in their ego's antics. No one ever wins, and no one ever has a chance to win—even those initiating the competition never truly win.

Counter Competition with Compassion

Conflict often appears as a simple invitation to engage in a friendly competition with a colleague, friend, or family member. If it's in good fun with healthy, mutual competition, then of course, go for it. I love a good games night! But you don't have to lose joy over something in which you were never meant to compete in the first place. When others invite discontentment and pointless competition, be direct in confronting the conflict. Combat challenging group dynamics with compassion. Yes, I absolutely did say "compassion." Counter competition with a compassionate approach. Decline to engage in a kind, generous way. I guarantee you that, whatever the conflict is, it's not worth losing your joy or contented, peaceful vibe over. Obviously, people who feel a strong need to always compete are dealing with greater underlying issues.

An article by *Psychology Today* lends us some insight to understanding those who thrive on competition. It says, "High-conflict people (HCPs) have high-conflict personalities. This means they have an ongoing pattern of all-or-nothing thinking, unmanaged emotions, extreme behavior or threats, and a preoccupation with blaming others." It goes on to say that HCPs may bully the people they target, and subject them to other confrontational behaviors. It says that, at their core, these people are afraid of being inferior or powerless, so they use this behavior to try and place themselves above others. Recognizing these distinct patterns of behavior equips us to show empathy for these people, while at the same time empowering us, through joy, to preserve our peace simply by not engaging in their antics and by staying in our own lane.

One way to reign victorious is to turn others' ego-driven competitions into an opportunity to engage in the power of joy, by complimenting, not competing. Compliment others instead of competing with them. Win at your own pace by implementing the energy of joy. When someone tries to get a rise out of you, rise up to the occasion, cool as a cucumber, and give them a kindhearted compliment. Distract them from their own egotistical games by crushing it with kindness.

You are in charge of your life and do not, in any way, need to engage in their ego-centric antics. Engaging in competition with other peeps is unproductive. Stay cool and collected by simply sharing a compliment with someone who sparks competition. Do not feel pressured to succumb to other people's ideals. Stay true to you. Taking the high road will lift you to become a high-roller in life. Success and respect will most certainly roll your way, too.

Envy Will Leave You Empty

We are all human, and envy can pop up and rear its jealous head even with the most cool and confident of people. So, in the same way we did with eliminating competition, reframe personal feelings of envy. Dilute envy with the uplifting energy of encouragement.

Encouraging others is a great way to run your own race. That way, you can eliminate any competitive emotions towards others. Use encouragement as a key tool to boost your journey with joy. Resist feelings of envy by rising above feelings of comparison and jealousy. Redirect your intentions to building others up. Although we might not want to admit it out loud, feelings of envy or jealous often stem from focusing on the personal traits we most admire about another person—but then our ego overrides our thoughts and drives us to envy. When we act from a place of comparisons, our admiration sneaks past our ego and turns our thoughts sour.

Eliminate comparison by replacing it with admiration. Turn your envy into an act of admiring. Why not benefit even from your misplaced resentments by reframing your thoughts of jealousy into a positive light? It's likely your resentments stem from something you value and want to seek for yourself. When you remove the negative energy associated with being envious, it turns into the positive light of admiration. Admiration is an advantage in becoming victorious. And victory always shines the light of joy.

Furthermore, building others up by paying them a compliment, through encouragement or by showing admiration, will (in turn) lay a foundation for your own, personal growth. It is when we truly begin to understand the art of running our own race that we free up energy to focus on our personal goals, and also to lead others.

The Joy of Mentorship

Leadership and mentoring roles are incredible opportunities to spread the power of joy to others while increasing our own internal energy levels of joy. A boom-tastic idea! Be a gift to others. Mentor someone who sparks potential. Encouraging someone else to shine is a wonderful gift that's in all of us to give. Kick start someone's dreams. Lifting someone's spirits today provides a seed of encouragement so they can soar tomorrow. Building up someone's confidence to succeed is a tool in running your own race. Tap into the success of mentoring on both sides of the coin.

Seeking out mentors is a lucrative step towards success, too. Always take opportunities to learn from others. Identify the attributes you admire about a particular person you look up to. It could be as simple as liking the presentation they just did—even that's a starting point. Then set a few goals in line with achieving similar accomplishments for yourself to thrive in that area too. Go a step further, and be a bold warrior spirit by reaching out to them via LinkedIn or another networking platform. Let them know you admire their abilities, and then ask if they would mind answering a couple of specific questions about their success that would help you master the same skill. See? Even envy can be used in a positive light to learn and grow. You only have one life to live, so don't waste a minute empty in envy or regrets.

Maslow's theory of self-actualization is a good basis for understanding how to run your own race. Abraham Maslow was a psychologist who said that, "Human motivation is based on people seeking fulfillment and change through personal growth. Self-actualized people are those who are fulfilled and doing all they are capable of. It refers to the person's desire for self-fulfillment, namely, to the tendency for him/her to become actualized in what he/she's actual potential. For examples, an artist who has never made a profit on his art, but he still paints because it is fulfilling and makes him happy."

Focusing on your own desires to live a life filled with joy trumps any abilities we feel we are missing. It's about what inspires us to soar.

Pace Yourself

Running your own race doesn't mean you actually need to run through life. Give yourself permission to slow down. Take time to breathe and enjoy life's little pleasures. It is especially important to cherish moments of joy when you lead a super-busy life. Burning the candle at both ends eventually ends abruptly, as it is extinguished by exhaustion. A busy-go-go-go lifestyle can leave you feeling anxious or overwhelmed, as if you never have enough time in the day. It may even leave you feeling like your life is spiraling out of control. Slow down your pace to gain control back into your life.

In our fast-paced world, it is very easy to get caught up in a self-defeating state of mind. Self-defeating thoughts leave you feeling two steps behind, or like you are running through life yet never getting any further ahead. As a wife, mom, fur-mom, small-business owner, writer, and life coach (to name a few of my everyday hats), I know first-hand that it's not always easy. But, if you make a conscious effort to slow down, even if only for a few seconds, to connect with the little things that bring you joy, you will be more productive and happier in your life.

Pacing yourself will help manage contentment in your life. Combat feelings of stress with a present-moment mindset. *This moment is the one that you are living right now.* Let the ebb and flow of the moment give you a freeing feeling of peace. Don't resist the progression of change or allow others to steer your opinion or agenda. Stop your spirit from streaming too fast. Challenge circular thoughts of defeat by asking yourself, *How true is that thought? How likely is it that this scenario will play out in my life?* Usually the answer is somewhere between, *Not very likely* and *It won't happen.* Don't lose precious moments in a self-defeating state of mind. Life pulls us in many directions at once, and it's understandable if we occasionally lose ground in the chaos. Make sure you pace yourself along the way, so you make it to the finish line.

All Seasons are Important

Like the tortoise in the story of the tortoise and the hare, you are exactly where you need to be. Stand up strong within this very moment to strengthen each moment thereafter. You deserve the grace to run your own race. Sometimes, we feel like we are being pulled off course, in a completely different direction than the one we'd planned. Or perhaps, your life has stalled like an old car, and you feel like nothing can jumpstart you back on track.

I am here to reassure you that things in your life haven't stopped. Everything in our lives is ever-changing. Some seasons may seem slower than others, but the exact same amount of time has elapsed in the slow seasons as in the apparently rapidly moving seasons of life. The slower seasons could be a pivotal development in your personal timeline. Only you possess the power to jumpstart a stalled season. It's your life.

A life-development stage sometimes gears up to catapult you in a different direction, one that will prove much more significant than you ever imagined. So, stay focused on doing your very best job in the slower seasons of life. These seasons hold just as much value as the fly-by-the-seat-of-your-pants fast times. The slow seasons are preparing you for the next big steps. Don't lose focus by being disappointed or distracted by the pace. Don't miss your destiny. The next season could be the most powerful one yet! It could be a season of exponential growth in all areas of your life. Don't race through the slower seasons. You might just fly by some amazing opportunities.

Enjoy the season you're in and do your part to recognize that each day is valuable by trusting the process. Acknowledge that acceptance adds value to each day, and simply do your best right where you are today. Keep this in mind on both the ordinary days and the more profound days of celebration.

Signals of Success

When you run your own race towards success, you have the ability to stay optimistic. You keep believing. You don't let negative thoughts negotiate your future.

You've got a spring in your step, and no one can bring you down, while you lift others with your positive energy.

You have an intent and willingness to help others, despite personal setbacks. Giving is a gift that lets your spirit rise with joy.

You don't get stuck behind others and sidetracked by their success, because your destiny is too important. You stay on track by refocusing on your own personal goals.

You have a work-harder, work-smarter, dream-big attitude that directs you towards success.

You move beyond your fears, or simply move forward regardless of fears. You just keep going.

As hesitation isn't always helpful, you don't second guess that you are deserving of success. You go for it.

Chapter Ten
Patience with Persistence

*"Surround yourself with the dreamers, and the doers,
the believers, and thinkers, but most of all, surround
yourself with those who see the greatness within you,
even when you don't see it yourself."*
– Edmund Lee

According to dictionary definitions, patience is a state of *endurance under difficult circumstances*. But more simply, patience is your ability to keep calm and think clearly during stressful times. It's your ability to wait without becoming anxious or annoyed.

Mastering patience is an important act of self-regulation that's vital to success. Patience is a key tool that will greatly benefit you in becoming successful in all areas of your life. Being patient will allow you to make better decisions. When you feel less rushed and more composed, you are more likely to be accurate in executing decisions. Patience takes the pressure off and gives you the grace to slow down for a moment to catch up. When we move too quickly through life, important decisions can be made in haste, and errors are more likely to occur. Being patient is a great pacing tool. Patience offers a calmer and less stress-filled life.

Patience aids in our relationships with others too. Self-control when frustrated with others is a tool to maintain harmony in both our personal and professional relationships. Showing flexibility, acceptance, and respect for others strengthens and empowers patience to thrive within us. Others might process things with a vastly different approach to you, but you don't need to follow them. By adding the element of patience into a situation, we open our minds to other ways of seeing the situation. Patience allows us to honor others' and their interpretation of the process, as well as ourselves.

We greatly benefit from the ability to adopt increased self-control via a more patient mindset. Patience allows flexibility to flourish in our relationships, fostering a stronger bond with family and friends—a bond that enhances the feeling of joy in all our lives.

In Patient Pursuit

Establish a patient pursuit towards living in peace. A patient pursuit is a delicate balance between the preservation of your personal feelings of peace and a consistency and commitment to forward momentum. Patience goes hand in hand with persistence. Persistence is the courage to keep going with optimism, despite your current circumstances. It's not always easy, especially during turbulent times, but it's always worth adopting a patient mindset while persisting in the pursuit of all you deserve in life. A patient pursuit will help you achieve set goals— perpetually moving towards success while holding on to a peaceful nature. Pace yourself with a patient pursuit that will inspire inner joy, even when joy feels distant.

There is calm allure as one moves in the direction of a patient pursuit. At times, you may feel like you are stuck idling in life, but in truth, it's usually in the patient times that we grow the most. You are still very much moving along, even in the seemingly slowest or less delightful times.

I've had many moments throughout my life where I needed to apply this principal. Directly after university, I was ready for the world and *so* enthusiastic to land that perfect job, but each perfect job I applied for didn't see me as the perfect candidate. I eagerly rolled along my peaceful pursuit of life, even as it presented me with one closed door after another. After a while, though, life started to lose its luster. I felt frustrated and sorry for myself. I did not yet understand the importance of persevering through the slow times. Instead, I started to blaming myself, wondering what I did wrong, looking at what I didn't have, and having a good, old pity party. Luckily, as he did when he inspired me to go to university in the first place, Jeffery held my hand as I stood back up on my own two feet. It's not always easy boosting yourself back up. Gain momentum knowing you owe it to yourself to keep going.

A person who continually pursues life with a purposeful intent, while carrying on in a composed nature, acquires a peaceful rhythm and a peacefulness that creates success on its own terms. You might not be fully in control of the situation, yet you still achieve a feeling of control through a heightened awareness of your own, inherent state of peace. Circling back to a patient pursuit, when facing much uncertainty, certainly has made a big difference in my life.

A Calm Confidence

Patience with persistence will increase confidence. It will create a calm confidence to work within a situation, rather than against it. That is the way to win when faced with any obstacle in your path. You will be able to view a situation with a more positive lens. You can embrace each moment, no matter how it randomly plays out, which will also reduce tension and stress.

Be mindful of what triggers the feeling of impatience. When you start to feel impatient about a situation, relax and take a deep breath. Focus on the present moment. Meditate on something that brings you joy. Take a ME moment to recenter and reframe your thoughts back into the moment.

A simple way to hold on to a state of patience is simply to distract yourself from what is causing the worry and anxiety that can come when you're waiting on something specific to happen, especially when it's something we have little to no control over. Simple steps to gain control in the moment will distract you from spiraling out of control while simultaneously encouraging you to live with peace and joy.

I learned this principle in my own life the moment I discovered I was pregnant with our first daughter, Savannah. While Jeffrey and I got married before any of our other couple friends, most of them started having kids before we did. (And comparison, back then, most definitely stole my joy!) Jeffery and I had decided to prioritize launching careers and building a home in the country before trying for kids, yet the hyper-competitive side I had back then made me crave having kids for myself—*even more*. So, deep down, I was envious of my mama friends—and yes, it did leave me feeling empty. I also consciously isolated myself from those friendship. Life's definitely a journey of discovery that I've since discovered how to win, with joy, by focusing in my own lane!

When Jeffery and I did decide to start trying for a baby, and it didn't happen within the first few months, I started stressing about it. It became less about fun baby-making time and more about, *Why the heck hasn't this happened yet?* No amount of love and gentle reassurance from poor Jeffrey could alter my attitude. I wasn't able to face the possibility that we would not have our own children. I had been adopted when I was a newborn, and although I had wonderful adoptive parents—who are indeed my real parents—I had always dreamed of blood relatives of my own. I was counting on mine and Jeffery's children to be my first ever blood-related relatives. That's a lot of pressure on my uterus and Jeffery, I know—not exactly the ideal mindset for success. Thank goodness I have cultivated a multitude of valuable life lessons, developing my positive mindset, since my early thirties!

After six months of unsuccessful trying, I even went so far and so fast as to take all the preliminary fertility tests. Everything came back perfect, so then I had Jeffery get tested too—he graciously accommodated my erratic request, even though he was feeling no personal concern or worry that we wouldn't conceive. All signs were positive, green light for go, and all my worries melted into heartfelt gratitude. My huge reframe resulted in a positive pregnancy test within a couple of months, and nine months later, I joyfully became a mom.

Mindset is everything. Once I switched to faith and released my fears, I was able to project that energy into the world, and it came back to me via my beautiful baby girl. My patient persistence is a practical pursuit that serves as and inspires much joy in my life.

I would find myself four-months pregnant with Sienna at Savannah's first birthday, and Liam would arrive before Sienna turned two years old—and when Savannah was only three years and four months old—giving us a big, beautiful family. My dreams of having a blood-related relative came true, three-fold, in three years! See how my many worries were wasteful? Staying in faith is the guarantee. When we can't glimpse into the future, we stay in faith, and we don't lose out on that time in the moment. I learned a valuable life lesson that I will never forget, and I heed its advice as I move on in life. I hope it will help you, too!

My birthing stories were anything but smooth sailing. Highlights include the following:

After thirty-six hours of labor, eight-*hour*-old Savannah, who had developed unforeseen health concern, was rushed *solo* via an ambulance to the ICU of a better-equipped hospital forty-five-minutes away; the hospital refused to let me go with her, and Jeffery was given the (only) option of following behind the ambulance in our vehicle. So, my very first night as a mother, I lay alone in a maternity ward, bible in hand, focused only on extinguishing fear.

Liam arrived two weeks "over-baked," weighing in at a whopping ten pounds, with *no C-section,* a day before our family was abruptly rerouted to a temporary home (*one third the size and two cities farther away*) for several months, pending unforeseen and extensive foundation repairs that the builder discovered were needed only days before we were scheduled to move into our intended and much-anticipated new home.

My unsurmountable faith gave way to unmeasurable strength. By shifting my energy towards a patient pursuit, I empowered a heartfelt commitment to keeping faith. And you unquestionably can too!

To Recenter Yourself Towards a Calm Confidence...

Take a few deep breaths.

Enjoy a ME moment to center yourself and relax.

Troubleshoot what's triggering feelings of impatience.

Focus on what you *can* control.

Distract yourself from feeling stuck. Make a list of achievable goals.

Reassure yourself, and then cheer yourself back to feeling peace.

Each situation that causes stress might be different, but the principle remains the same. Slow down your pace, take action steps towards keeping cool, and hold on to your peaceful joy.

Patience is present when you can successfully pace yourself. Self-regulate your thoughts to stay in the moment. Keep calm, and don't let the small stuff distract you from achieving your goals.

Evaluate as you go. Ask yourself, *Does this current event truly impact my ability to move forward?* If the answer is no, then simply keep going. Small steps still move you forward.

Treading in deep water makes us stronger swimmers. Even though we aren't physically moving anywhere, the motion increases our stamina while conditioning us to thrive within the water. You might feel like you're treading water in life, not really getting any further ahead, even though you're working hard. In truth, you are learning and growing stronger, even if you don't notice it right away. Thrive in life with a patient pursuit towards success. Remember that each step evolves at a different speed. Standing in one spot doesn't mean you're not moving forward. Take pride in your patient nature. It's a skill that not many master in life.

Patience Happens Behind Closed Doors

Patience and persistence. Practice these two key ingredients to lead a successful life. I read an interesting article that described patience as being exhibited not on a public stage but behind closed doors, like a father telling a fourth bedtime story to his daughter, or like an athlete waiting for his injury to heal. When we go out in public, it's always the impatient ones who catch our attention in the form of grumbling customers in slow-moving lines and drivers honking in traffic. There are many movies that acclaim the virtues of compassion and courage, but there are few movies that speak about patience. Take moments of pride when you act with great patience in a challenging moment. Believe in patience as a powerful tool to maintain your joy. Be proud of your patient nature. Patience is a true, learned mastery over the self.

Clarity comes with patience. Perfection can't be rushed. When you take mindful moments of time to focus in—to truly capture a unique vision of beauty, as if through the lens of a camera—you must first patiently fine-tune your focus. Be patient in the moment as you do this. It's in the silent, still moments that we gain most of our strength.

The skill of pacing allows us to manage various productive activities with a stress level maintained at an optimum range. Although they are not as famous in our society as they should be, pacing skills are necessary when we encounter social, physical, mental, and emotional limitations.

Regular exercisers and athletes know the worth of cooling down and warming up, both of which are pacing skills. They prevent injury and can help you stay in the race for longer. Similarly, entrepreneurs daily come in with an increased level of energy, which is often followed by periods of recreation, relaxation, and rest. They pace themselves for long-term success.

Perpetually experiencing stress at uncontrollable levels is definitely not healthy. Regulating your pace will decrease stress in your life. Focus your attention on staying in the moment and breathing. Take one conscious, deep breath. Living in the moment is one of the best ways to feel in control of your pace in life. Tackle the day one moment at a time. By shifting your thoughts and making a conscious decision to live in the moment, your stress levels will automatically start to decrease.

Sometimes, we are dealt unfair situations that dictate our pace in life. We must seek ways to rise above our urge to simply stop, or give in to the feeling that we are failing. We must also stay patient in the process, as time corrects the troubles life has dealt us. Patience isn't easy for anyone. It's a true skill to master, yet a patient mind holds the power of inner peace and joy.

Jeffery's ability to set his personal pace dramatically changed after his injury. It's precise and accurate to say that, before the injury, Jeffery was extremely successful at everything he tackled. So, to suddenly feel trapped in a state of constant head pain and suffering from debilitating symptoms like memory loss, insomnia, and light and noise sensitivity required all his patience. Yet, with Jeffery's unbelievable determination, warrior spirit, and patient pursuit, he made it through the unquestionably toughest twenty-seven months of his life.

Your Own Path of Patient Pursuit

Below are ten action steps towards success. Use them to design a step-by-step plan to stir up your own success.

1. Identify your goals.
2. Be positive; always keep believing in yourself. Never give up.
3. Ask yourself, *Why not today?* Act now. Don't wait until tomorrow.
4. Envision success—make a clear, detailed picture in your mind of what success looks like for you.
5. Write down easy, achievable goals.
6. Hold yourself accountable by scheduling touch-base sessions with yourself to evaluate your progress.
7. Be encouraging, not discouraging. Press the reset button if you haven't yet reached your goals.
8. Celebrate small victories along the way.
9. Focus on the possibilities, not the problem, and you will find a faster solution.
10. Keep striving towards success with an exuberant intent to thrive.

What are you determined to accomplish today? Take time to reflect on and determine what you want from your life. You set the pace!

Grace to Win the Race

Grace will find you. Be open to receiving grace by recognizing that *you deserve good things* in your life. Believe you are worthy of abundant love, peace, joy, and much success. When something unexpected happens, pushing you off course, always believe in second chances. Stay determined, and stand strong in your faith that this surprise path will take you towards new opportunities. When we are open to learning along the way, the possibilities become endless. So, be open to new possibilities. Approach yourself with grace. I'll make you a deal: I promise to see the best in you, if you will too!

You have value regardless of how many connections you've got on social media, or whether you have an expensive car or a multi-million-dollar home. And you are unmistakably no less valuable if you've made mistakes or haven't reached your goals . . . yet!

Choose to wear a medal of honor wherever you go, one that shines brightly out from your spirit by way of how you show up in life. Don't let life's challenges define your direction by wearing a victim's badge. Instead, adapt and progress through new challenges with the grace god has given you. Grace is bestowed on us all. It provides the strength to maneuver with faith. It was a strength I needed as I trudged through the depths of our challenging circumstances. Grace is forgiving, and grace is divine. My grace and faith wouldn't allow me to be distracted from accepting joy into my life. You need to boldly welcome joy too!

Race Check Point

Remember, envy will leave you empty, so jump beyond jealousy by redirecting your intentions to build others up. Choose compliments over comparison. Eliminate endless comparisons by giving someone a compliment instead. Crush them with kindness; then everyone is a winner. Establish an alliance between your mind and spirit to cheer yourself on, overriding self-defeating thoughts that slow you down. Stop fretting over failure. Instead, release past failures from your thoughts to free yourself up for success. Failing is not fatal. Failure is not your final story. Be inspired, not intimidated, by someone else's success, and adopt and emulate traits that you admire about the other person. Pace yourself by promoting a present-moment mindset. Take time to center yourself back in the moment. Do this with grace and faith, and you too will never be distracted from accepting joy into your life.

Chapter Eleven
Faith Over Fear

"When fear knocks, let faith open the door."
— Joel Osteen

Questioning my faith is like questioning my existence. Faith is the foothold to my resilience, forming a foundation within my heart to bind love, hope, and joy as one. It's a solid entity that endures infinitely, allowing me to conquer my greatest fears. Faith acts as a canopy, shielding me from my greatest hesitations and doubts, while at the same time providing unbreakable strength to help me leap beyond fear-based reluctancies.

No matter what it looks like for you, faith inspires an authentic freedom for mind, body, and soul. Let faith free you to capture joy within this very moment.

Time wasted paralyzed by fear is more terrifying than fear itself. Time is a gift given to us all, and this extraordinary gift emerges in the form of a brand-new day. Time is our truest blessing to be treasured—exactly like a precious gift. We can lose much time in life being anxious and fearful, wasting precious moments living exclusively in a fearful mindset and feeling hopeless. Fear creates a limiting belief, which gives the impression that we are helpless. Fear is an innate human emotion, and none of us can escape its grip. However, an attitude of faith can loosen the constricted feeling that fear holds over our life. Honor yourself by holding on even tighter to your faith. Faith will rescue you from feelings of fear. Reframe fearful thoughts with faithfulness, which will recover feelings of hope and redirect you towards a faith-filled future. Combat fear-based thoughts with a plethora of faith and a present-moment mindset.

Act on Faith

It's one thing to carry faith in our hearts, and quite another to act on our faith. We must be actively engaged in faith-driven thoughts. Acting on faith equips us to overcome our greatest fears. Form a deliberate and determined consciousness around being an active participant in faith. *Activate* your faith by being a *big* believer in all that you do. Reluctancy will leave the recipient of your faith—be it God, the universe, or whatever it is that gives you strength and guidance—reluctant to deliver all the amazing things that are in store for you. Never doubt all the great things that faith can make happen in your life. Activate your faith to discover the astonishing things that are in store for you. Believe in yourself triumphantly. Acting on faith creates bona-fide freedom for your soul to experience all the greatness that is intended for you.

I am a self-proclaimed biggest, big-time believer, acting on faith with the intent to thrive with the glorious glow of God's greatness. My personal faith is in Him. As you can imagine, Jeffery's traumatic brain injury brought on relentless and debilitating symptoms that tried to weaken and discourage his spirit, and at times, left us feeling hesitant and fearful. Any bit of sudden light or noise would send Jeffery's pressure headaches spiraling out of control. Not one of the doctors and specialists—and we saw plenty—could find a solution to the relentless pain plaguing Jeffery's mind.

For me, calming the fears took an unfathomable amount of faith. It seemed like our life had forever changed from a fun-loving family who gratefully enjoyed the best of what life had to offer to suddenly being a family who kept the blinds closed in a house with floor-to-ceiling windows designed to welcome every ray of light. The injury and its symptoms were determined to dim our light of love.

The first six months proved to be especially tough, with so much change in an instant. The injury left us startled, like a deer's gaze caught in a car's headlights, frozen in the middle of the road. While Jeffrey consistently experienced varying degrees of head pain, he continued to act on his faith. The greater his warrior spirit fought feelings of fear and uncertainty, the more visibly victory and healing became apparent. I am so very thankfully he acted on his faith!

I believe in you, and I believe you deserve an abundance of joy. Act on your faith, whatever that is for you, and embrace the many joys you deserve in your own life, regardless of the challenges you're facing at any given time. You're worth it! Believing I was worth it gave me an inner strength to rise up to the challenges in my life. And you can have that inner strength, too!

Faith Is the Invisible Guide

Even as we felt completely displaced from our former life, as though we had walked through a door to an unrecognizable world, acting on our faith continued to be the number-one way we championed through to a season of recovery. I say "a season of recovery," because much like faith, even though we couldn't see it, recovery and healing was happening at every moment.

Faith sets our true warrior spirit free to soar above our fears. I encouraged my family during this season with a warrior stance, remaining strong and genuine, for I knew faith would guide us through, while our unconditional love would cushion the impact of adversity. In the past, God had always blessed our family with a strong love, staying by our side through many challenging circumstances—mind you, never a trial of this magnitude. We felt protected, with the Lord's strong presence truly lighting our path forward.

At every turn, we acted on our big-believers faith by valuing every opportunity to alleviate Jeffery's symptoms. We definitely experienced moments when we questioned whether Jeffery would heal. This happened when the neurosurgeons acted more like counselors, encouraging us to keep positive and stay in faith while providing no timeline or actual remedies, and while we tried everything from allopathic doctors to homeopaths, naturopaths, neurologists, pain specialists, acupuncturists, chiropractors, psychologists, psychiatrists, friends, family, and even the advice of well-meaning strangers. But through all that, none of our doubts could sway our faithful hearts.

Faith as a Tool for Stepping Forward

Acting on faith was a key tool to keeping our joy while we listened to everyone's advice on how to treat the symptoms of a traumatic brain injury. Each step was an amazing act of patience with persistence at work. We explored a private clinic, graciously provided by the company where Jeffery was employed. One of Jeffery's employers called in a favor to the head of a prominent hospital in Toronto, and we got so excited, hoping for some amazing insight or state-of-the-art treatment. But when the hospital's chief doctor called, he told Jeffery to just keep hope, be patient, and stay encouraged as the brain will repair itself in time. He said, "You're young and strong. You should start to feel relief and heal one day." Even faced with this ambiguous and unhelpful reassurance, we chose to focus our thoughts on faith. We faithfully stepped forward in the hope that the next recommendation would provide a more solid path to a solution.

We acted on our continued faith by engaging in various remedies and treatments, and maintaining optimism in the moment. We did whatever inspired a positive vibe—anything to distract Jeffery from his head pain and other debilitating symptoms. We faithfully waited, and waited some more, learning the valuable skill of patience with persistence. Patience, persistence, and pacing are important for keeping your faith, as well. And eventually, healing happened, magically, over time . . . by holding onto faith and tapping into the power of joy. Faith and moments of joy were the only things I knew for certain would lift our spirits, so we used those tools, and I was lucky enough to bear witness to my amazing husband's healing—a blessing of our faith indeed.

Faith is a factor in everything we do. Faith gives us an alternative to feeling lost. Faith acts as a new direction. Like a GPS navigator, unwavering faith finds a new path and re-roots us back in that comforting feeling of home.

Fearlessness

Empower faith's ability to work by pushing past your fears. Faith is an awesome phenomenon, and acting on faith is a game changer. Engage in faith to see yourself soar to new levels of success in all areas of your life.

Faith over fear is a trusted slogan that reminds us that faith is more powerful than our fears. Fear is an emotional response, while faith is both emotional *and* logical. Depending on who you ask, faith is *primarily* thought to be logic-based. I only know that faith lifted me up to thrive, while fretting in fear made me feel trapped in my troubles. I'm always choosing faith over fear! This doesn't mean my fears are any less scary. I just won't let fear run my world.

Everyone experiences feelings of fear. Some levels of fear are actually good. Fear can light a fire within us to take action. It gets our adrenaline pumping. We can offer tremendous acts of faith with much fear in tow. But fretting in fear creates deeper issues by raising a negative perspective, bringing on feelings of anxiety and stress. And the most debilitating symptom of a fear-based mindset is that our fears don't leave room for faith. When we're reluctant to connect with faith and believe in ourselves, we continually let fear drive our thoughts. With the absence of faith, fear remains the front-runner in your thoughts, driving you to explore only the negative slant of every event or circumstance.

We need to keep faith in the driver's seat of our thoughts. Let faith fuel your thoughts to rev-up a positive perspective. Letting go of fears will allow your faith to move fires out of your path. Let your faith shine brighter than your fears, leaving your thoughts unavailable for fears to take root in. Your mindset determines how you move forward in life, not your circumstances. It's your choice to make faith your *first* choice.

Move forward freely with faith. Our ability to fuel our thoughts with faith is simply magical. Faith can magically lift our spirits to soar over the most challenging moments in life. Faith gives us the strength to keep going by not only facing our fears but also *surpassing* them to become victorious. Be a winner with faith driving your dreams.

Use Faith to Thrive

Faith is my greatest tool for thriving in all circumstances. Faith lifted me up, so I could encourage Jeffery throughout his recovery. Connecting to the importance of faith in healing is instrumental in guiding us towards holistic healing. Holistic healing, for us, was allowing our spirit to recover from the disruption, as well the physical recovery. Some people hold onto hurt long after their physical ailments have healed. They won't let go of the sorrow they felt in losing time to physical injuries. As they hold the hurt, they continuing enduring negative emotional losses, even though they have recovered from the physical setbacks. Now, they're missing out on more precious moments that they could be pursuing to enjoy their best life ever. Use faith to set aside fears and regrets.

Faith is the strength we relied upon to boost our spirits. Keeping faith is simple, yet not always easy. You need to stand strong in faith and not let your fears knock you down again. Act on your faith. Be actively engaged in a faith mindset. Nothing was easy, but faith was simply the only action that I accepted in my heart. I constantly reframed doubts and fears back to a faith-driven mindset. You need to be consciously aware to keep your faith.

Be deliberate in your faith and maintain a positive mindset. Unwavering faith, love, and joy will prove to be victorious, so hold onto hope and what you can control in the moment. So much of our control is left up to time and circumstances. Hold tight to simple pleasures that bring you joy. Make the conscious decision to take back control wherever you can. Let faith set you free.

Don't lose faith, especially in the tough times. Most often, in shared stories, it's during the difficulties that a foundation of faith evolves our spirit to strengthen. Move forward with confidence that each experience, good or bad, will aid in launching you forward even stronger and more resilient. The hardships you've faced have helped lift the limits you put on yourself. This proves truest when faith is present.

In times of uncertainty, fear will be your biggest enemy. Faith must work twice as hard to override our fears. We regained our footing and stayed in control by keeping our faith. I truly never doubted that Jeffery would be healed from his injuries. My faith simply wouldn't let me doubt his recovery.

Our circumstances left us riding across a wave of uncertainty driven by fears, including a fear of the unknown. Our situation left us unable to react as we may have done before Jeffery's accident. We were clinging to faith as each wave hit higher than the last, yet never seemed to peak. At times, we felt helpless but never hopeless. We would not be at the mercy of our troubling situation. We took back control, and sometimes that's all it takes to begin to feel peace in a sea of uncertainty, or a calm amidst the crashing waves.

Developing My Faith

For me, an immense connection to faith developed in an extremely unconventional way. While my adopted and truest parents always encouraged me to believe in God, they never formally instructed me with one particular religion. As a child, all I knew was that we were Christians, Jesus loves me, God was good, and I needed to try my best to be good too, to receive his love. While, on occasion, my mom would sporadically get bouts of energy to attend or try a new church, the novelty wouldn't last long.

My parents encouraged my free-spirit—and left seeking religion up to me, I guess to establish my own ideologies and discover a personal connection to God. And although I dearly love both my parents, I don't believe a child or even a teenager should be expected to filter through so many layers to understand how to be one with the Lord.

Through the years, various friends and family members invited me to churches with them, and I was always eager to explore a greater spiritual connection. I found myself attending a Hindu temple with a friend and her family, and even wearing a sari. I sang alongside another childhood friend who introduced me to the Baha'i faith. I loved and would often sit on Sunday mornings with my grandmother as she watched Reverend Robert Schuller preach on the television. She was the one constant source of pure genuine encouragement in my life as a child, so I took great heed in learning from her incredibly wise insights and talents.

In my early twenties, I even took a brief yet keen interest in the Church of Scientology after I received a copy of L. Ron Hubbard's book *Dianetics: The Modern Science of Mental Health* from a member flogging them on the corner of Yonge Street in Toronto. The book launched the Scientology movement—and my brief interest in it. I subsequently spent time at the Church of Scientology in Hollywood,

California, exploring their beliefs and discovering who I was, before swiftly moving in the opposite direction.

Then one random day in my mid-twenties, there was a knock at our door, and two well-dressed young men asked me what sort of relationship I had with God. All I could say was that I always felt God loved me. I hadn't explored first-hand much beyond that idea. For a small donation, they left me a copy of a daily bible, immediately prompting me to start exploring. I read it religiously, pardon the pun, until I had finished every word. I made notes with a pencil and marked pages with sticky notes along the way. I discovered how deeply God loved me for me, with all my perfectly perfect imperfections and fabulous flaws. I felt a first-hand and amazing closeness to God, for I understood his intent to love, lift, and protect me. Although I wasn't even baptized at the time, I gave my life to Christ.

Though each of my escapades in discovering my spirituality, I always felt the love of God. He stood by me through all my moments of self-discovery, never wavering even once.

Today, I love listening to Joel Osteen, an American pastor and acclaimed author, who luckily for me, has his own station on SiriusXM radio. Joel also has weekly, televised sermons, which have been seen by over ten million viewers in more than one-hundred countries. Joel lends me much encouragement, and I am grateful for his service. Jeffery first discovered Joel while flipping through the television channels just after we had moved to Arkansas. I walked in while he was watching Joel one night, and I haven't stopped listening since.

Everything Joel spoke about, that first time I heard him, resonated with me on so many levels. I enjoyed the uplifting encouragement and his fun, authentic approach to delivering each message. I am a big fan of Joel and his wife, Victoria. They offered inspirational, faith-driven encouragement that, after the accident, sometimes became the primary boost of joy and positivity in my life.

God is *my* greatest connection to faith. I have faith that, each day, God lifts, loves, and validates us with his unconditional love, which each of us deserves. I believe that God wants us to reach out. He wants us to know that we can have a one-on-one relationship with him, and that we can be as close as anyone else in the world to his heart. He loves us all equally, and his love lights every part of my life. For me, God is the essence of an abundant, glorious love.

Faith is faith, a powerful tool—so whatever makes up the foundation of your faith, hold it closely to your heart. That is where you will find your joy.

Spark Light in the Darkness

Validate the thoughts, worries, and stresses that stem from a fear of the unknown. It's absolutely understandable when you're feeling overwhelmed and facing new challenges. Fear makes you feel unsure about the future. These types of feelings come up for all of us. Our reaction is the key to staying connected with joy. Decide how you will move forward. Warrior through with a positive mindset, or suffering through as the victim, takes the exact same amount of energy. I want to encourage you to take the warrior mindset, and spark light in a dark situation.

To connect with your inner light, validate and understand how you're feeling. It's okay to not be okay. Understanding how your feeling empowers you to move forward. Be aware of your emotions, for addressing your emotions helps you release feelings of fear. Knowledge is power, and thus, we need to stay informed. We need to actively find answers to any and all questions circling in our thoughts, and subsequently seek the solution.

What is your specific concern in the situation? Seek the answers you need to ease your worries. That being said, make sure you're finding balance between being informed and still taking joyful moments throughout the day. Seek new possibilities and don't dwell in the problem. Focusing only on the doom and gloom will surely increase your feelings of fear. When fear and anxiety creep in, switch to feelings of gratitude and stay patient. I know it's not always easy, but you're worth it.

Moving beyond fears fuels courage and confidence that stays in your spirit forever. Sparking light in a dark day will allow you to shine, even on the darkest of days. Let self-love be the spark that lights your heart. Be present in this moment, and grateful for this day. Leave regrets in the past, and ignite your flame of faith every day.

Trust in faith. Trust in yourself. With so much turbulence and uncertainty in our world, we need to open our minds to trusting the process more than ever. Change is inevitable, yet we waste precious energy resisting change. Embrace faith to flourish. Be faithful in everything you do, and remember that joy inspires faith to flourish freely.

Chapter Twelve
Present Moment Mindset

"Do you not dwell in the past, do you not dream of the future, concentrate the mind in the present moment."
— Buddha

In my early days of motherhood, one piece of advice I frequently received from parents with older kids was this: "This time will fly; so, hold on to each minute, or before you can blink, they'll be all grown up." I took their advice seriously. I tried my best to be mindful and adhere to their kind-spirited advice. For as I am now realizing with each passing day, that advice comes from a heart longing for a glimpse of those precious, beautiful moments before their own young children grew up so quickly.

As a newborn baby, I was put up for adoption. Growing up, I always held a bit of curious-wonderment in my heart. I longed to experience the phenomena of a biological connection—a person with a similar genetic makeup and shared unique traits. And as every parent can relate to, adopted or not, my heart could never have imagined such an immediate and immensely overwhelming joy and love for my children. My heart felt the wholeness I'd craved for as a child.

I always feel extremely blessed to have had three beautiful, healthy babies born within three years and four months of one another.

My three extreme blessings had me extremely busy, but as I look back, I recognize distinct moments that I made more special by engaging my energy in the moment. Embracing each moment made it easier to stay focused on what mattered most—as best as I could.

And that's all I am encouraging you to do. It's not always going to be easy, but as we talked about in chapters three and four, I guarantee it will be worth it. You will find more joyful moments popping up in your life—moments that will boost your spirits. Permit the sun to shine into your spirit each day, simply by cheering yourself on within the moment. Become your very own cheerleader. You are doing an incredible job simply by trying your best! And if anyone tells you any differently, send them my way. I will fiercely defend how incredible you are. And I can do that by stating the facts: You're rising above negativity simply by engaging in the moment and choosing to spend time reading this book. That's all I truly need to appreciate your intention for joy.

Honoring Your Inner Voice

We touched on the present-moment mindset earlier in this book, but I want to devote this chapter to it, so we can explore its power in letting us live a joy-filled life. When we are truly in the present moment, the purest pleasures of inner peace awaken a soothing silence, a *peaceful* silence, rendering the spoken word as an unnecessary interruption to listening to our truest intent. When we cease to speak, our internal voice comes through in the rhythm of our soul, reawakening us to unearth our deepest truths—truths that allow us to move forward freely in the very best direction.

Our hearts connect with our thoughts to shout out in a blissful silence. Our spirits start to feel whole again when we're deliberately living in the moment. This wholeness is only made possible by a present-moment mindset. We can freely seek new opportunities in the moment, knowing that nothing impedes our path moving forward.

The inability to hold a present moment mindset leaves our thoughts scattered amidst the past, present, and future, spreading fragments of our thoughts twirling in many different directions. Imagine you have a small cup filled with water. You can see, feel, and taste the water with ease, all contained within the cup. You can even hear the water if it were to trickle into a second cup. Yet, when you pour the cup of water into the ocean, it loses all distinction. The water from your cup is now completely dispersed into the vastness of the ocean.

The water from the cup is much like our thoughts, distinguishable when contained in the present moment, but easily dispersed into the ocean of past perplexities or the expansiveness of the future. Then it's no longer easy to live in the moment. Our thoughts start twirling in different directions, and we lose our sense of peace.

Collect your thoughts back into the moment. A present-moment mindset actively disrupts any distractions by refocusing our attention back onto what's contained in the immediate minute. Channeling your thoughts to inspire a present-moment mindset is a key tool in achieving your best life.

Not the Past, Not the Future

Timing is everything. All we can truly count on is this exact moment in time. Holding your attention in the moment will not surrender a minute or let you miss out on new opportunities, because your thoughts are not circling backwards and/or spiraling forwards. Focusing too much on the past or future will inevitably distract you from experiencing joy and feelings of happiness in the present moment.

Let's leave future predictions to the weather app. Don't let negative thoughts downpour on your day. Although usually quite unintentional, our discouraging thoughts can cast a negative cloud over our own lives as we remain fixated on the rain. We must make an effort to become aware of the sun's perpetual presence. Although we may not see the sun, it is most definitely behind the clouds, even on the darkest, stormiest days. Never lose sight of the potential of a rainbow emerging in your life.

A rainbow is first seen as the sun slowly peeks through the clouds. A balance of storm and sunshine is needed to evoke the magical beauty of a rainbow. Sometimes, we focus too much on predicting what could go wrong, and in doing so, we ignore the fact that the situation could be getting better. The sun could be starting to come out, and life could just as easily go right. And in most cases, life does work out for the best.

Don't let a negative mindset steer you towards predicting the future as anything less than the very best. Narrow-minded assumptions can lead our thoughts on a journey down the wrong path and in the wrong direction. Limiting beliefs limit our progress in life. Live stronger with a limitless mindset.

Our past replays as fiction, and our future is merely a prediction. This means you can never truly reclaim the past. Be it truth or fiction, you can't go back and change history. That part of your story will not alter, so you must come to terms with the past to move forward freely. Forgiveness frees you by letting go of the hurt. Instead of replaying the past in your thoughts over and over again like a broken record, embrace the past as part of who you are. Like it or not, the story remains the same, so don't waste precious time pondering past mistakes or misgivings. You might accidentally press the replay button and relive something you would have preferred not to repeat. And the power of suggestion is powerful indeed. Let a present-moment mindset prevail to enhance your future successes, and let it be a future filled with the excitement of new opportunities.

The future is unknown—a mystery to us all. However, the future is inevitably destined to continually evolve as we move into each new chapter of our life. So, unless you have a magical crystal ball and fortunetelling, clairvoyant skills, please don't waste precious time trying to predict the future.

Use the present moment to drive your future in the direction you want to go. Focus on following achievable steps towards accomplishing your goals.

The Incredible Benefits of Mindfulness

Mindfulness is simply the act of being in a present-moment mindset. A clinical trial published in the JAMA Internal Medicine journal showed that mindfulness meditation significantly improves sleep. The trial focused on participants with existing sleep-disturbance conditions, and studied the way that mindfulness affected their sleep patterns and how their daytime cognitive function changed as a result. In the short-term, mindfulness helped participants to sleep for longer and benefit from deeper, better-quality sleep. And they were more alert and responsive to cognitive tests during the day!

An ever-increasing number of studies show that mindfulness has the power to prevent physical illness, and to aid in faster healing. Ryan McKim's 2008 research paper gives us a great example. In an eight-week mindfulness program, participants experienced less pain and illness. The paper said, "In that calm state, you embody a sense of safety, knowing that you are not under any immediate threat. So the body can focus on crucial restoring and healing work." That's an amazing insight, and it's one of many incredible benefits of mindfulness.

Living in the present moment frees us from our fears, apprehensiveness, and inhibitions, extinguishing feelings of self-doubt. We promote a heightened sense of courage and confidence simply by taking advantage of every minute. You deserve to not miss a minute. Be mindful, and make every minute count.

A Mediocre Mindset

Resist the temptation to settle into mediocrity. A mediocre mindset will prevent you from achieving your greatest dreams in life, limiting you from reaching your full potential. It's just that simple, sweetie! Strive for more because you deserve more. You deserve to be living out your dreams! So, go grab 'em!

Mediocrity is a limiting belief, one based in general terms and on an average assumption. Mediocrity is established on the premise that ordinary or average is okay. There's no real desire for greatness or a feeling that you deserve much in life. But I'm here with all my joyful energy to set the record straight: This is simply not the case. No one deserves to live in mere mediocrity. Truthfully, you deserve all the desires you've ever dreamed of. Each star is a dream, and you deserve all the stars in the sky when you've wished and worked hard for your dreams to come true. Each dream—each star—deserves at least a chance to shimmer in your life.

Mediocrity isn't defined so much as bad; it's just nowhere close to the super-abundant greatness you deserve in life—a super-abundant greatness that you should be aspiring towards.

You Are a Superhero

"Heroes rise above the mediocrity that surrounds them." This quote offers us a great example of being your own superhero simply by rising above a mediocre life. Recognize that you deserve more than mediocrity. You deserve the honor of being a superhero, one who stays focused on achieving your dreams, working passionately, and striving beyond barriers to accomplish greatness in your life.

You are fantastically fabulous! Beautifully bold! Cunningly courageous! You are a superhero! Start acting like it today by embracing the power within you. Embody greatness simply by believing in yourself. Carry on in life with a fearlessness as you aspire to become your very own hero, even if, initially, only within your mind. Mindset is everything!

Everything in life needs a starting point, so start today by imagining you are a super-abundant superhero of greatness. Your confidence will shine bright and attract a gleam of light from fellow superheroes. Your astonishing powers include your ability to adopt joy and a *best-life-ever* mindset. You can see success through any adversity, while always believing in yourself. Having a positively powerful mindset encourages you towards an unlimited potential to thrive. You've most definitely got this!

Our mindset determines how we show up in life, so adhere to your own superhero status. Capture the essence of your inner hero. Manifest the idea within your thoughts. Manifest a true warrior spirit, a hero of courage and confidence, someone you can be proud of. Define your strengths and powers by showing up each day in that very light, one that illuminates everyone you encounter while lifting them closer to their own superhero status!

Become the brightest star. Superhero status will grant you the freedom to fly high in the direction of your dreams. Jet forward in life by recognizing your true worth. You are one of a kind. You offer the world a unique prospective that can't be duplicated. You are a gift to us all. Hold this notion in your heart. Adopt these encouragements as yours. Own them with confidence, as they reflect who you are in the world. Take flight as a hero who is a strong, true warrior spirit. Claim super hero status simply by believing in yourself.

Lights, Camera, Action

Be a star. Lights, camera, action! You are the *light*—release your gifts to illuminate the world. *Camera*—envision the very best version of yourself and capture it in a still-shot of your imagination. *Action*—take bold achievable steps towards your full potential. Every step along the way is valuable.

Self-discovery is an inside job, so look within your heart to identify what drives your spirit forward. Gravitate towards what brings you most joy. Once you tap into pursuing your passions, map out a plan, move forward with star-confidence, believing you possess an inner greatness to elevate your life to new levels. Level up with a success mindset.

We can't all be good at everything, but recognizing our strengths and gifts by pursuing our passions is important to living our best life ever. Everyone falls into varying categories of mediocrity, and this is perfectly okay. We all won't get the chance to be stellar athletes, scholastic superstars, world-renowned actresses/actors, or praised painters. We must leave something for others to do! However, everyone is indeed gifted, and every one of us most certainly deserves to shine as bright as a brilliant star in the sky. Shine brightly by releasing your gifts out into the world and shine with pride. Do not dull your shimmer with thoughts of perpetual lack or limiting beliefs about yourself. Don't give into a mediocre mindset. I see big things happening in your future, so please stop the *"I'm not good enough"* self-talk.

Sweat, struggle, and shine. Be prepared to sweat, as it is going to take commitment, hard work, and grit. Nothing worth working for in life isn't without struggle, but push past the struggles to shine successful. Shine brightly, knowing you've done your very best to drive your dreams forward towards a successful life.

Shine Up to Your Full Potential

All that being said, avoiding mediocrity can be a tricky balancing act, and it can even trick you into believing average is your only option. A mediocrity-mindset lacks luster, so in turn, you feel your life lacks any shimmer. Your lack-filled thoughts dilute your spirit's shine, simply by thinking you don't deserve more than mediocrity. Don't believe the hype. You most definitely deserve to shimmer and shine!

Envision a shiny penny, shimmering in the sunlight—a perfect penny perhaps once used by a magician to inspire a magical moment. Then imagine a tarnished penny darkened with age, faded, and barely recognizable. Shape and size are the only mutual traits that identify it with its shiny counterpart, but we will make the assumption that it is, indeed, a penny too. Let's presume these two pennies were produced at the same time, in the same mint, and of course, both represent an equal value.

As a child, I loved the magic of randomly discovering a penny. It was a treasure of luck that inspired joy. I loved saying, "See a penny, pick it up, and all day long you'll have good luck." I deeply believed in the good fortunes of serendipity or anything else prompting a joyful moment, even as a young child. I would be through-the-moon excited to randomly happen upon a shiny new penny and would hold it in high regard. I placed much more value on it than an old, tarnished, all-worn-out, seen-better-days type of penny. As a kid, I might have even kicked the old penny aside, not valuing it in the same light as its shiny equivalent, and forgoing my chance for a lucky day.

Although both pennies are worth the same amount of currency, their value was interpreted very differently in the eyes of the beholder. Even though both pennies started out shiny and newly produced in the exact same timeframe, their experiences in life left their external appearances very different, causing labels and assumptions to form, and setting the pennies apart in stature as viewed by others. This mirrors how we see ourselves and shines a light on how we value our own self-worth.

How do you see yourself? Have you tarnished through time, or are you still a shiny penny? How we view ourselves reflects how we allow others to treat us, so are your experiences in life tarnishing your shine?

Everyone is born a beautiful, shiny new penny. Over time, life's hardships can dull our vision of our true self-worth. We lose the ability to recognize the beauty of our shine, and sadly, our spirit starts to tarnish, and we begin to feel less worthy of all the splendor we started off believing we deserved. We stop investing in ourselves until a shadow of failure clouds over our shine. Don't let unfair situations darken your future days. Start renewing your shine today! Reinvest time in self-love and self-care. You deserve to see glorious gains in your life!

You are valuable. You have resiliently risen above difficulties. Don't let life's challenges tarnish how you perceive yourself. You still have the exactly same worth. A shiny sense of self-love will reveal your truest value as priceless. The price you'll pay for discounting your truest worth is extremely costly. It's a debt that damages your self-esteem and diminishes your confidence. Believe that you are a shiny, bright, beautiful, new penny.

Mindset is Magical

Have you ever wondered what it would be like to have magical powers, like a mystical wizard who possesses spectacular abilities to manifest your own dreams to come true? It's a miraculous idea to imagine: a wonderment of joy created in our own mind. A creation of our own thoughts can truly be magical. Ultimately, the magic behind all our dreams coming true has little to do with mystical wizardry and plenty to do with the magic of mindset. Our mindset holds the power to design or destroy our dreams. Be a dream designer, a fashionista of faith and of the profound possibility to spark magic in your life.

Design your dreams with positivity, determination, and a never-give-up attitude. Destroy dreams with negativity, discouragement, self-doubt, and a fear-fueled mindset. Make up your mind which of these two options you'd like to move towards. If you can boldly, beautifully believe in yourself, you will (in turn) boldly, beautifully believe in the magical power of your own thoughts. Our thoughts hold a powerful influence on directing us to achieve our dreams. The wizards' wands are optional. Simply stated, a positive mindset has the ability to manifest magical momentum to make your dreams come true. It's a magical potion that drives your dreams forward.

Embrace an Abundance Mindset

Your mindset is filtered through a spectrum of colors. Let's imagine white represents a scarcity mindset, where you believe there's never enough money, time, love, or whatever, and an abundance mindset, where you think there's plenty of everything, is represented as black. These two polar opposites are both extreme perspectives. There is a rainbow of colors in between those two.

A person with an abundance mindset focuses on the numerous opportunities that are available in life and business. They prefer to focus on the positive aspects in life, rather than negative ones. Having an abundance mindset makes people more creative, more grateful, and more focused on collaboration. As a consequence, they attract more creativity, people, and opportunities into their lives. They live more harmoniously and are more emotionally organized than those who are victims of stress and trauma. So, believe in the magical abundance of life, and manifest even more abundance for yourself. I want that for you.

You Are Magical

Believing in yourself will sow seeds for your dreams to take root in your heart. Your heart nurtures your dreams to grow by way of self-love. Loving yourself is the greatest act of believing. Always believe you can do anything you set your mind on. Faith is the foundation for all our dreams to come true.

I dare you to believe that *you are the magic in the moment*. We've already discussed how our thoughts are magical, so believe it, and you will become it! You *always* have the opportunity to be the magic in the moment.

There was a short window of time between our family's season of recovery and the COVID-19 pandemic starting, but we made the most of every minute. We experienced some magical moments traveling to our favorite, oceanside destinations in (you guessed it) California. I had the good fortune to visit twice during those seven months between Jeffery's recovery and COVID-19 restricting our travel options. I accompanied Jeffery on his first work trip to the States since the accident, and then we took the kids for the American Thanksgiving holiday, when we enjoyed a magical vacation to the most magical place on earth: Disneyland!

My son, Liam, magically celebrated his tenth birthday there, building his very own R2-D2 in the new *Star Wars* themed section of the park. We tried churros for the first time! They tasted magically delicious! Back home, we hosted a haunted house-warming party over Halloween, complete with a magician who mystified everyone in attendance with a show and tricks to celebrate the magical feeling of settling into our fifth and final home in three years! Joyful family moments inspired by an unmistakable cascade of magic.

Yet, for me, nothing is quite as magical as the laughter of my beautiful children, usually provoked by some good-humored teasing from their fun-loving father or a clever joke told by their witty grandpa—comedic relief definitely runs in the Cunningham family.

Our kids' laughter illuminates my heart with joy. Any other mama would surely agree with me, for no matter where we are in life, the magic of our love is our greatest blessing. Love unifies us as one throughout the universe.

And without question, laughter elevates our joy factor in life. Ever notice that it's almost impossible not to laugh or at least start smiling when someone else is laughing? It's one of the reasons sitcoms use a laugh track (strategically placing audio laughter louder at key times to prompt audience laughter). It works—proving that laughter really is contagious. The magical sound of laughter resonates synonymous with joy, all around the world. Laughing evokes much more than a happy moment of feeling joy.

Countless scientific studies highlight the multitude of health advantages laughter perpetuates. Discoveries have shown that laughing triggers the release of endorphins—as noted earlier, endorphins are considered one of our body's happy hormones. Laughter improves our mood and increases feelings of relaxation, while at the same time relieving stress and anxiety, magnifying our resiliency, and helping to combat chronic pain.

These are just a few of the amazingly-awesome health-boosting benefits of laughter. So, let's get laughing—immersing ourselves in a magical state of joy, simply by seeking ways to increase laughter throughout your daily routine. It is a hilarious way to seek joy every day, and I guarantee it will put a smile on your face.

Magical moments can happen at any time, because you possess the key to unlock the magic in your life. Enchant the world with your miraculous zest for life, leaving others to conclude that someone as happy and full of joy *must* be magical. Magic stems from a willingness to believe in something more than the physical. When you watch a magic show, you start to believe in the power of magic, and in turn, enjoy the performance much more than the person sitting in skepticism with arms crossed and a sour face of disbelief. It's the person engaged in every fun-filled moment, watching in awe and cheering with joyful delight who is the true magic of the show.

You are the magic in the moment. You have the ability to bring magic to each moment just by showing up with joy, leading with love, and by interacting with others in a positive kind-spirited and compassionate way. Your outward, blissful manner will mesmerize even the most reluctant individual. Be magical in every moment, and you have the freedom to live a miraculous life.

Being empowered by positivity allows you to embrace magical moments. A positive outlook also lifts your spirit with a magical light that's only available when you adopt a positive mindset. Believing in yourself releases a magical spell to illuminate your life with joy—*the light of love*—while enchanting others with your kindness leads you to shine brighter with compassion. Share your magical love with the world.

Every trial in life tries strongly to unravel magic. It's not always easy to see magic through the lens of life's harsher realities. However, it's the discomforts in life that most encourage us to work towards our dreams. We must lend insight to both sides, light and dark, to balance the magic and the darkness of the world and achieve a harmonious life balance.

To truly live a balanced, magical life, you must remain open-minded, always believing and striving for the best in life. What you think really will drive you forward. Happiness psychologist Shawn Achor says, "It's not necessarily the reality that shapes us, but the lens through which your brain views the world that shapes your reality." This means that, altering our scope, we reshape the outcome and direction to be distinguished in a different light. The circumstances did not change—merely our outlook. Reformulate your thoughts with faith, and watch happiness and joy shine brighter in your life.

Even when our current reality seems bleak, we start to adapt to our environment out of necessity. We stop engaging in the possibility of our dreams coming true, and can get stuck in a rut. Imagine you start a new job simply to pay the bills. It's okay in the interim but should be viewed as temporary. Often, though, you shift into long-term thinking, imagining yourself in that dead-end job forever, and robbing yourself of your dreams. Or, you make plans with someone simply because they are available, yet you don't enjoy their company. You hold strong to the idea that you have no other choices in life, no one else to be friends with. All your false, limiting beliefs have conditioned you to keep hitting the repeat button in your mind, leaving no room for a dream job or a fulfilling friendship to pop in as an option. You need to stop believing that your current circumstances are your final story. If you felt differently about yourself, then you would value the time alone, and make room for magic.

Reignite the magic of your dreams by maintaining a positive, optimistic, dream-driven mindset, one that owns the idea that anything is possible. This is essential to ensure that you don't stand in your own way of living your *best life ever*. A joyful mindset is just as easy to manifest as a negative, doubt-driven frame of mind, and guess which one will lead you to success in all areas of your life? If you answered anything other than *"joyful,"* then it's even more awesome that you are reading this book. But for all of us, I cannot stress enough how important it is to establish an encouraging, positive, magical mindset.

Chapter Thirteen
Lead with Love

"Joy is a net of love by which you can catch souls."
— Mother Teresa

Self-love is very important to living your best life ever. Make sure you don't stand in the way of your own happiness, with self-sabotaging thoughts or a self-defeating mindset. It's simple: A loving, positive frame of mind will bring joy into your life and so much more. Self-defeating words—the kind that don't come from a place of love—limit you from reaching your full potential by actually sabotaging your success before it can even surface in your life. Positivity comes from love. Positivity is powerful.

This is simple in theory, but definitely not always easy. Consistency is key in applying a loving positivity to all areas of your life. If you consistently strive to defeat against negativity with a loving, positive attitude, you will always surface in success.

That sounds ideal, but in reality, there are many distractions trying hard to pull you down with negativity and make you feel a little less loving towards life and even yourself. It's no wonder that we can get caught up in a struggle to stay positive, but your warrior spirit has lovingly got this!

Self-Love Tips to Combat Negativity

Stop in the name of love—self-love! Stop listening to the negative dialogue inside your head. Our thoughts manifest who we become, so mindset is everything! Here are some tools to combat negativity and give your warrior spirit a glow that, positively, will leave you beaming in love—self-love!

Self-Evaluation-

A simple self-evaluation is an exercise in self-love. Reflect a moment on your lifestyle choices. Are they aligned with your values? Are they affecting your ability to move forward? Are they slowing you down from achieving your goals? Are they helping or hindering you from living your *best life ever?* Take time to evaluate where you are and the choices you're making. It's never too late to make changes. You are in control and always have the opportunity to move yourself forward.

Honoring yourself

Being proud of your achievements is an easy way to show yourself respect for all the hard work you have done. Honoring your accomplishments isn't arrogant. It inspires confidence, which boosts your spirit to step past fear and leap towards your goals.

A Love Letter to You

Make sure what you're telling yourself is as dreamy as a love-letter, each word written with much intentional love and sincerity. Romance yourself into believing every immaculate truth. You go throughout your day listening to the words you speak about yourself. Make sure you're telling yourself the right things. If you are positive and saying great things about yourself, then you are likely to have a great day, not because everything is perfect but because you are confident that you are loved and cherished, regardless of what others may say.

Declare Your Love

Declare your love to yourself by taking time to nurture your mind, body, and soul. Self-love and self-care are essential tools to living a joy-filled life. Work on developing self-love. Treat yourself by indulging in relaxation before you get burnt out. Make sure your thoughts cheer you on in life. You are lovable, and you owe it to yourself to live a life feeling loved. Go ahead, I dare you to be your own number-one fan.

Invest Time

Investing time in yourself and what brings you joy is a confident act of self-love that creates an important foundation for your own personal growth and success. It also gives your spirit the strength to support others. My self-confidence stems from my unconditional self-love, which allows me to confidently lead with love in everything I do.

See Yourself As Successful

Create a mindset where you can already envision yourself enjoying your successes. Manifest success from within by believing in yourself. If something knocks you down, stand back up twice as strong, knowing you can always draw on the inner strength of joy. Make sure what you're telling yourself is what you want to see happen in your life. Do not listen to the naysayers; they're only spectators in your life. Listening to them will distract you from achieving your goals, and they will steal your joy.

Show Gratitude

Showing gratitude for your accomplishments is an act of self-love. Being grateful is an easy way to add love into your life. Celebrate all your blessings. Feel deserving and accept when good things come your way.

A Jubilee of Love

If love were a party, I'd be celebrating with the world. Join me, and let's celebrate actioning love together! Celebrate each day with the intent to explore a more loving side of life. Leading with love shines a light on compassion, respectfulness, peace, and global unity by sharing a genuine concern for others throughout the world. So, let's get out onto the dance floor and bust-a-move together, inspiring a world jubilee of love. Let's celebrate and get excited about love.

Dreams by Design

Imagination sparks a dream. Dreams are seeds that were planted in your heart, perhaps first cultivated when you were only a child. But it's going to take more than waiting for them to grow into your reality. You must keep nurturing a dream by feeding it faith, and being patient and persistent—sowing the seed, so to speak! Our dreams only evolve into reality when we do our part in making them come true. Dreams don't just magically appear out of nowhere. That is a miracle, not a manifestation of a dream.

Of course, a miracle sounds like a great route to success. Yet, what you are losing in a miracle is the fact that you are not doing your part towards achieving your dreams. The process is important. I might even argue that the process is *key* to truly achieving your dreams. Without working through a process, you can't fully appreciate what you receive. Absolutely, some of us will have to work harder than others to achieve our dreams, since everyone's capacity and experiences are different, but that in no way means that dreams cannot be achieved so long as you work hard while working smart.

We do this by keeping our focus on the present moment and doing the best we can where we are standing. Each step prepares us for the next one. This helps blossom our spirit to grow even more. I want you to get introspective and ask yourself this: *What are you doing to pursue your passion and accomplish your dreams? What steps are you taking towards success? How will you grow your seeds?*

No plan? No worries! Take time to identify what success means to you, and you will have an enlightened approach to lasting success. Make a plan by articulating your thoughts, and creating steps towards your goals. And when I say "a plan," I mean a realistic plan with achievable, set goals, and specific dates and times in place. Without specificity, you won't work hard. If you set a time frame, you will be more likely to achieve your goals. That is how you will reach towards wherever you want to go in life. Design your dream, articulating every dynamic detail. Always stay determined. Don't detour from developing your dream to come true! Let your imagination design a decadent dream to take deep root in your heart, one you can take much pride in through the process of achieving it.

Designing My Own Dreams

One of the dream seeds planted in my life turned into one of my greatest accomplishments. It was a dream I didn't even know I truly wanted until I was in my early twenties: the dream of becoming a university graduate. Before I met Jeffery, I never even knew this dream would one day take root and blossom through to success. When I meet Jeffery, he was a school scholar, fiercely focused on his academic career. He asked me why I wasn't keen on pursuing post-secondary education. I told him it wasn't anything I'd ever even considered. True story.

I struggled through my school years, scraping by with low-yet-passable grades. Subjects like art, music, and Phys-ed kept my interest and average up—all of which I enjoyed! Although nothing ever materialized in way of a formal learning-disability diagnosis, time was spent in elementary school trying to figure out why I wasn't achieving higher academic success, but no one *ever* took the time to teach me how to study or what applying myself in school looked like. I never understood how to organize my academic time or made school a priority.

This continued right through to high school, where my parents encouraged me to enroll in general courses, which were considered easier than advanced ones, further separating me from feeling confident. The academics side of school definitely wasn't a priority for me. However, I more than made up for it with the social side, always looking for that harmonious balance, even back then. To say I was a social butterfly would be a spot-on assessment of my fluttery, fun-filled high-school experience. I dropped out at the end of twelfth grade, *just* before gaining my last few credits to graduate. The following semester, I enrolled in a young-adult program with a couple close friends (who enjoyed the same joyous social schedule in high school) to earn my last credits for completion. One friend, *Erin* remains a forever bestie—completing the ICF coaching program by my side, a true confidant and cheerleader as I wrote this book.

One of my high-school teachers did plant a seed to take root in my life, encouraging me to consider a career in modeling. The power of suggestion is powerful, so that is exactly what I focused on for a few years before exploring all my options. I wish I'd known then what I know now: All of our *options* are infinite! Sometimes a dream is waiting in the wings for you to discover it. Unfortunately, we can get distracted by focusing on "Why not?" and let "Why not me?" lay dormant. Let self-confidence awaken the courage to unlock all the dreams you deserve. Nothing less!

Jeffrey continued nurturing my seed to enroll in a post-secondary program by encouraging me with the possibility and the positivity he spoke over my life. He told me, "You're just as smart as anyone I know, if not smarter. You deserve the same opportunities as others. There's no reason you can't go to college or university." It was in those moments that all the limiting beliefs were lifted, and the seed for success in that area of my life blossomed into a whole garden of possibilities.

I accepted Jeffery's statement as the truth and never looked back. Although I initially had to jump through a few more hoops to get myself into university, I did just that. I enrolled myself into the pre-university program at York University, which I was very thankful they offered to mature students. I knew it wouldn't be easy, and it wasn't. I worked my butt off, studying and focusing, and I pulled off amazing grades, graduating with a bachelor's degree in sociology and a minor in women's studies. This is something I have been proud of my whole adult life. It's never too late to discover a dream. Start today!

It's Never Too Late

Never stop pursuing your passions in life. Understanding what those passions are is as simple as knowing what excites you, what motivates you to work hard, and what keeps you up at night dreaming and planning for a bigger and better future. These are your passions. These are the dreams in your heart.

They might be simple to identify, but they are not as easy to achieve, because for that, hard work is required. It takes determination, commitment, and continued faith to reach the top. You need to always believe in yourself—dreams take determination, dedication and discipline, *all doable!*

I believe that directing our attention to our goals and dreams brings us much joy in return. When we focus on our passions, it evokes a bright ray of joy that illuminates our life and opens our heart to multitudes of possibilities. The possibility that anything is possible if you work for it is a beautiful thing to experience. Focusing on your dreams increases joy, and then the journey itself doesn't feel like work. It feels like an exciting trail that will get us to our light. And that is why I implore you to design a dream in your heart; let it bloom with possibility, nurture it, and refuse to give up on it.

Since we are talking about dreams here, I'll take you back to childhood, when our little brains were just like a plain canvas. At night, in our dreams, we painted those canvases with exciting fantasies, and in the morning, we excitedly rushed to transfer them to real canvas. Back then, this used to be it. But I wonder, today, why I was never told earlier that my dreams were worth more than just being painted on a canvas. Why was I never told, "Don't stop dreaming, for that is what real life is?" Why was I never taught to dream big, because I deserve a life of choices?

A Dream Is a Game Changer

Today, standing in this phase of life, I realize that a dream with passion can certainly be a game changer, because it helps us know *why* we want to achieve what we want. To achieve the dreams planted in your heart, you must understand how to make changes in your life to increase your joy and success while achieving those dreams. In understanding who you are, you understand the direction you need take, and the road you have to travel down. For that, you must explore your heart, because the destinations are limitless. If you can dream it, then you can do it as well. You already possess the most important element: your dream. It is the seed that you need to nurture your determination, love, and hard work in order to see your dreams grow into your reality.

And for that, again, you need to make joy a priority. Having joy in your life is a matter of greatness, because joy in your heart brings joy to your actions, and when your every action is filled with joy, you exude a positive image that is loved by everyone and anyone—most importantly, yourself.

Affirmations for Showing Self-Love by Following Your Dreams

Always be in a seeking mode to find that pot of gold at the end of the rainbow.

Abundance is out there right now. You just have to go get it!

Be a dream catcher.

Go out and catch your dreams.

Put actions behind your dream.

Plan goals to achieve your dreams.

You are unstoppable.

You are invincible.

Keep these affirmations in mind and repeat them often as you start showing yourself true love by honoring your dreams.

Chapter Fourteen
Passions Are Popping

"Passion is energy. Feel the power that comes from focusing on what excites you."
– Oprah Winfrey

Oprah Winfrey needs no introduction, as an iconic multi-talented influencer of excellence in our era. I watched *The Oprah Winfrey Show* religiously for twenty-five enlightening seasons. I adore the Oprah Winfrey network, OWN, and *currently* love *The Oprah Conversations* on Apple TV. Ms. Winfrey inspires us to recognize how we can impact the world, highlighting the importance of our collective contributions. She leads by example to be *"Positive Impact Makers."* Ms. Winfrey's authentic encouragement prompts my passions to pop!

Pursuing my passions is exactly how I came to write this book. There was an amazing sense of purpose around sharing my experience with the enlightened energy of joy. I knew God had placed the strength of joy in my heart, just as he is placing these words of encouragement in your heart to cheer you on too. I am simply a humble messenger, sharing tips and tools that worked to strengthen my connection with joy.

The decisions to become a life coach and to write this book illuminates my life like a double rainbow lights up the sky. They're awesome examples of passions popping. It's the pursuit of our passion that leads them to pop into our purpose. I had zero desire or motivation to go back to work, yet I ventured out of "retirement" to train for a year to gain the knowledge and credibility required to become a certified life coach (although my heart already knew I was positively passionate about encouraging others to embrace the power of joy well before my accreditation).

Today, I sit in a silent state of reflection, rejoicing for a moment on the awesome direction my life has taken. I'm not exactly sure how everything guided me onto this incredible path, but I am extremely grateful that it did. Within days of obtaining my coaching certification, I started my own business, JoyINC, and began seriously writing this book.

The magical power of pursuing my passions propelled me to achieve my goals. A straightforward, innate drive continually launched me closer and closer to my dreams. I could never have imagined what an immense blessing it would be to hold joy in my life. In my journals, I have composed several more sight-lines of joyful encouragement, which are waiting to bloom into books. Understanding your passion will help the energy of joy flow forward to flourish in your life, too. Pursuing what sparks passion in your spirit allows you to grow and blossom into everything you've imagined and more.

Your mind awakens with confidence in contemplating possibility as you hold a posture of pride and embrace the power of positivity. Your spirit stirs your senses as you start to transcend through a sensational season of success. Your five senses are captivated by your passions popping! Begin exactly where you are in this very moment. Get excited about your dreams. Dream bigger than anything you've ever imagined before! And let your passions pop.

Discovering Your Passion

Discovering your passion in life isn't like solving a riddle, nor is it a scientific problem that you have to work at. It actually takes very little brain power, if any at all. So, if you're here, wondering what your passion is in life, I suggest you explore your heart. Our passions lie within our heart only. It's super important to connect with what you treasure most in life. Of course, family and friends top the list for most of us. But let's explore deeper. Let's shift our thoughts and recognize what puts a spring in our step. What in particular makes us shine bright? What brings us joy? Perhaps, you already know the answer. Maybe you know what that passion is and are pursuing it. If that is the case, then it is amazing!

Your passions will pop up randomly and inevitably, so don't struggle another moment to understand what your passions are in life. Simply follow your heart, and it will lead you towards pursuing your passions in life. For many people, their passions don't appear with the pulling powers of a g-force. Sometimes, it's the most subtle signs that have the greatest impact. We need to be open-minded, take the time to see the signs, then take steps to act on your discoveries.

Don't let logic stand in the way of discovering your passions. Our practical scope on life sometimes prevails, and we don't take the opportunity to experience the more passionate side of life. Taking a more passionate approach in life will help you lead a more joy-filled, thrilling life.

Think about what sparks the most joy in your life. Make time to explore your passions. What do you love doing? What types of books do you enjoy reading? What do you like to do in your spare time? What makes you jump for joy in your life? Then take action, and try out those ideas for a bit. You don't need to necessarily quit your day job right away. Make sure your passion is the right fit in terms of time and energy, but never stop pursuing a passionate way of living life.

The reality of life has drained most people of their passions. It conditions us to not dream. It conditions us to be subservient, and do what others are doing, leading a boring life without passion. So, I want to ask you this right now: Do you want to truly discover your own, personal passions in life? Do you want to break the chains, and love yourself and your dreams, no matter what? Do you want to see your dreams turn into reality? Then I suggest only one thing: Get passionate.

Get Passionate

There are various opinions on whether passion follows purpose, or purpose follows passion. I feel that your passions can be pursued as a purposeful venture in life, but the fact is that both our passions and purpose are not as parallel as some may assume.

Since the time of ancient Greece—when Aristotle articulated his thoughts on the paradox "which came first the chicken or the egg"—countless philosophers, scientists, and genealogists have been left in a circular debate over the truth to this puzzle, with seemingly no end or resolution. I believe the same circular stance can be taken in this much-debated question: "Which comes first, the purpose or the passion?"

The Greek philosopher Aristotle introduced the ideas of *potentiality* and *actuality*. For example, the purpose of the egg is to become a chicken; the egg is therefore a potential chicken. The hatched chicken is, well, the actual (or actualized) chicken. Through a complex argument involving the perishability of anything potential, and the eternal idea of the actual chicken, Aristotle deduced that actuality always comes before potentiality.

According to Aristotle, the actual chicken came before the potential egg. The chicken versus egg question has come to be used as a metaphor for self-perpetuating cycles and the futility of trying to decide how the cycle began, instead of dealing with the cycle in the present.

Although passions and purpose are distinctly different, there is no reason why they can't become equally integrated in the process of pursuing your goals. It seems clear to me that my passions are indeed purposeful. I cannot imagine one without the other.

If you've already connected to your true passions in life, that is absolutely amazing! It truly is! My hopes and prayers are that you are purposefully pursuing your passions in full throttle, and that they evolve into living your *best life ever* while proving a gift to us all, as you share your strengths with the world.

However, if you're still wondering or even struggling to understand your passions, please don't worry a moment longer. You are not alone. Many people spend countless hours trying to figure out their passions. Living life with joy is a great start to discovering your true passions. Take action towards joy in your own life, and move yourself towards your passions. If we were talking to Aristotle, I believe he'd say that joy is the chicken and passion is the egg; joy comes first.

Ambition Is Action

Ambition is about moving *towards* success, and achievement is about focusing with hard work on your goals and dreams to *see* success. It's not about competition. It's about *action*. Make sure you're actively taking steps towards your dream.

Remember: Whatever you are most passionate about drives your ambition in life. Never stop. Keep taking steps towards truly discovering your passions in life. Sometime logic stands in the way. Sometimes practicality prevails in our thoughts and prevents a more passionate approach to life. But let's make it simple. Simply live in the present moment. Always believe in your dreams, as they were placed in your heart for a reason. Use your intuition; that tiny nudge knows which path to follow. Live a balanced life. Stay optimistic and keep taking steps towards what truly bring you joy in life, and your true passions will surface with ease.

Healing from Hurt Strengthens the Heart

When you've been hurt, strengthen your spirit by opening your heart to healing. You need to recognize and feel your truth to heal your heart. And for that, you need to validate your feelings, because you can be upset in the moment but have to be careful to not get stuck there. You deserve to give yourself as much time for healing as you have spent hurting. Hurting happens, but make sure there's room for healing too.

Allow yourself to feel emotions because holding on to them can hurt more in the long run. Allow yourself to heal from the hurt that you have experienced throughout your life. Holding on to feelings of hurt only paralyzes your spirit, preventing it from moving forward. Although we don't have control over hurtful situations in life, we are in total control over how long we remain a victim. It's your choice whether or not you allow your heart to start healing. Ignoring your feelings is suppressing your spirit from shining.

You have to open yourself up to understand how your emotions are affecting your ability to connect with joy. Joy is all around us, but in order to experience it, we must first be open to receiving joy. When we are in a state of unbalance, we are fully surrounded by negative energy. This energy rapidly takes over our mind and soul, when we don't validate our feelings, and subsequently our hearts are left heavy with sorrow. Balance yourself back towards center by accepting and moving forward with positivity. Begin to heal and feel like you're living a balanced life again.

Prevailing Over Negative Self-Talk

In my generation, parents taught us children not to talk back. Even as adults, for the most part, we tend to not engage in altercations simply to keep the peace, and more importantly, because it's usually not worth losing our joy over. Well, when it comes to negative *self-talk*, I'm telling you to talk back! Talk back with positivity to counter negative self-talk. Let positivity prevail.

Try to become aware of negative thoughts when they seep into your brain. Analyze them. Are they coming up because you are hungry, tired, disappointed, or anxious, or is it something else? There are many times when we ignore negative thoughts, yet they latch onto us like a parasite, not going away, and spinning a pessimistic slant on our ideas. We need to identify and remove these freeloaders from our thinking.

Make your inner voice speak to a negative thought. Tell it, "I will identify a negative thought and recognize that it is just a fraudulent story that I keep telling myself. In reality, there is zero truth to it, and therefore, I can stop the circular thought process from stirring up false, self-defeating stories." Separate yourself from the self-sabotaging narratives that are most definitely slowing you down from achieving your *best life ever*.

Positivity Initiates Possibility

Hypothetically, what do you do when you *want* to contract a contagious virus? Given the COVID-19 pandemic, we all have a very real and first-hand answer to this question. You would stay around people who are already infected with that virus. Of course, in reality, you would want to do anything possible to distance yourself from contracting the virus. You would place clearly defined boundaries to keep yourself safe.

These exact actions and advice need to be applied to hanging around toxic, negative people. It's easy to drift along, hanging out with your peeps, even if they don't have your best interests at heart. Most of these people don't think about anything but themselves, and you're just a means of getting what they need. They have no care or consideration for how you're feeling or what you need. That's not a friendship. That's a parasitic relationship!

It sounds harsh, I know, but these are the cold hard facts about people who just don't care about anything but themselves—people whose negative, manipulative mindsets can cause you to feel emotionally empty by draining your good spirit of optimism and drive. It might be your best friend or maybe it's just a casual acquaintance at work, but either way, you've got to set clear and present boundaries to protect your energy. Yes, your energy and feelings are very important. You are a VIP! And you need to start treating yourself like one!

These peeps aren't necessarily bad people. They are just having a bad effect on your positive vibe in life. If you feel like they are draining your energy, and you need to make a change, boundaries don't have to equal conflict. You don't have to ghost or completely eliminate them, but just create the space you need to be great. You need to make space so their suffocating energy doesn't affect you.

These people are the opposite of optimistic. Surround yourself with people whose energy is positive, peeps who lift you up, even if that person is you! Sometimes it's better to be on your own than to be caught up in a toxic relationship. This is an act of self-love. Give yourself breathing room, so toxic friends can't suffocate you with all their needs and wants. Space is grace. Give yourself time to evaluate which way you want the friendship to go.

Signs of a Toxic Person

Toxic people, generally, are:
- Joyous in jealousy. It isn't a form of flattery.
- Queens of control. Controlling you does not show that they care.

- Master manipulators, always pulling strings to get exactly what they want, while somehow, making you feel guilty in the process.
- Condescending con artists. Nope, it isn't very nice to point out other people's flaws and weaknesses, and yes, you definitely do deserve better. Seek out sweeter peeps!
- Selfishly self-centered. They do not care about you and your feelings. They are only focused on themselves and what's in it for them.
- Conquerors in conflict. They blow everything out of context and get crazy upset with you at the drop of a hat. Real friends share their feelings and come to a resolution; it's called healthy communication.

Focus on those who've got your back, not those who talk behind it! Good friends don't lie, put you down, or get upset at you for no apparent reason. If you find that behavior in a so-called friendship, pick up your hat and move on. When you don't have their cloud of negativity looming around you, it will allow positive peeps to see your shine! You've got this. Small steps still move you forward.

Perfectly Imperfect

What do you consider the perfect life journey? The ideas will be unique to us all, and there are no wrong answers. When you start your journey, there are going to be moments that will be debilitating and will rob you of happiness. But your vision and your passion to reach where you want go, and achieve what you want to achieve, will refuel your resilience to keep you going forward, even during those most challenging times.

Our path isn't always going to be perfect. Pebbles of discouragement or boulders of sorrow might have knocked you down, but get back up again, because the higher power of your dreams will lead you along your ultimate path. So, don't sweat it if your path is filled with hurdles. Take great strides with faith and leap over every obstacle that dares to cross your path. You need to strive for your goals by focusing only on the end state, and not on the hurdles in your way. And if you master that, your life will feel liberated, because you live on your own terms.

One of my greatest heroes, the beloved American television host Fred Rogers, said, "As human beings, our job in life is to help people realize how rare and valuable each one of us really is, that each of us has something that no one else has—or ever will have—something inside that is unique to all time. It's our job to encourage each other to discover that uniqueness." You are perfect exactly as you are in this very moment. You are perfectly imperfect. The meaning of perfection is subjective and a very individual idea, so make sure you are empowering your perfect self by honoring your uniqueness with true acceptance.

We might start to question or even blame ourselves for not striving harder for the perfect live, when in actuality, perfection is perfectly flawed. Flaws expose the raw truth of who we are—a truth that comes into focus with a much higher resolution, providing us a clearer picture of our truest self . . . an enlightened truth knowing it's authentically you!

When we identify our true self, we then begin to separate ourselves from the critical, circular thoughts that needlessly scrutinize our past mistakes or lay judgmental depictions of the future. Our glitches make us great, so don't let your differences define you as less than perfect. You are perfect just the way you are! Own an attitude of being perfectly imperfect, which is the most real perfection any of us will ever truly know.

Our own thoughts can actually blur our vision. It can feel like our minds are unable to move past our shortcomings. Discrepancies circle in our thoughts, telling us we're not good enough, we are different, and different is bad. Societal cues suggest we must fit in or be considered misfits, and we must aspire to the same path as everyone else to recognize true happiness. So, we're left chronicling the past and discouraged about our future, which is simply not a productive reasoning on which to base predictions about whether or not you can truly live your best life.

You Are Fabulous

Yes, indeed, you are fabulous! Own being fabulous simply by being true to you. Meet yourself where you are in the moment with a genuine admiration and much self-love. Take a moment to evaluate and recognize whether what you're telling yourself is inflating or deflating your spirit. A nagging, negative dialogue in your mind will only suppress your spirit. Consciously reframing negative self-talk to something fabulous is freeing. Build yourself back up by breaking down any myths or misgiving you have told yourself over the years. You are fabulous, so separate yourself from the false truths. Stop the circular thoughts of shame and the self-defeating words. Restart with encouraging words:

- You are fabulous.
- You are enough.
- You are lovable.
- You are deserving.
- You are stronger than the situation.
- You are empowered by connecting with the energy of joy.

These are simple truths, so believe them!

Make a promise to yourself to love every bit of you! Yes, every little lovable bit! Once you begin to recognize how incredible you are, you will feel an unconditional love take hold of your heart. Start to accept yourself as fabulous by virtue of your flaws. Joyously give yourself permission to simply adore yourself. By embracing yourself exactly as you are, you release the harmonious strength of joy, allowing it to flourish freely. Free yourself to feel fabulous.

Our First Love, Self-Love

Early morning is a great time to start to think positively. Have a morning ritual of positive affirmations, chant, sing, or say wonderful and loving things to yourself. Spend time loving yourself. Make a plan to maneuver throughout your day with the all-empowering feeling of love. Visualize your dreams and set some self-care goals for a successful day. It can be as simple as taking fifteen minutes on your lunch break to read your favorite book, or treat yourself to your favorite aromatherapy-infused bath before you go to bed. Have different small actions of self-care every day. Executing self-love as a priority is an amazing way to generate joy!

Love Is a Powerful Tool -

Let love strengthen your day. Love is a complex emotion. It can mean different things depending on who you ask, but most people agree that love is a powerful feeling of affection that empowers you, fueling your thoughts and emotions every day. Similarly, the power of love drives feelings of joy.

I have a love-at-first-sight, real-life love story of true soul mates. Jeffery and I created our love quite literally at first sight when we met under a moonlit summer's sky. The magnitude of my love grew exponentially as each of my three children were born. The power of love is the most profound act one can decide on, and no one can escape its transcendent power. Even a love lost is one of the most significant events of your heart and soul. Love is the essence of why we are here, and only a scorned heart can deny this unavoidable desire. Lean into love. Embrace love as the ultimate goal. And always start with self-love.

Love is the essential ingredient for success in every area of life. Your heart beats rapidly as it refuels with love.

When love doesn't work out, the circumstances may be heartbreaking, but you should never let it break your spirit or discourage you from loving again. Always believe you deserve unconditional love. At times, that love comes from within your own heart, and it is a true love that can stay with you forever. Love, from yourself or another, is an adventure that dips and dives. You just need to keep exploring to find your forever love. Fill your cup with love.

Sincere love is judgement free, though at times we must express *tough love* via a pure and honest approach, steering loved one towards their safest route or best directory in life. Leading with love, by accepting others simply as they are, will bring forth an abundance of joy in both of your hearts.

Self-Care Activities

Have a look at your life—the commitments, people, and activities you prioritize, and the way you spend your time. How many of these help you feel like the best version of yourself? How many of these don't? Which can you eliminate? Then start adding more things that can bring you happiness, be it spending time outside with friends or engaging in a new hobby. Identify the things that make you *unhappy* and see if those things can be removed. If they are in your control, then you can remove them. If not, then you can bring them down to a tolerable level. You need only to preserve those things that elicit joy, and you can renew your mind by decluttering your thoughts.

Once you start taking care of yourself, it will automatically improve your cognitive ability, mood, and overall functioning. There are different means of self-care for different people. It can be as simple as fifteen minutes of a morning routine followed by a good breakfast, cataloguing a to-do list, hitting the gym, and then having a relaxing shower with your favorite music while running a diffuser for added harmony. *Sign me up too please!*

Don't get discouraged if life happens upon your blissful intent to self-love—the doorbell rings, the dogs start barking, your sweetest-ever son or daughter spills the latte they so carefully and proudly carried to you, as a meaningful gesture, to bring you a cup of joy. Cue tears (it doesn't matter whose). Simply take a deep breath, then hit the reset button. That's the truest gift of a brand-new day: a fresh new start to reset your life! Self-love grants infinite chances to make life right, and heck, look at all the unconditional *love* along the way!

Enjoy the journey, as each day is valuable. Don't postpone making time for yourself. Carve out time each day for a little self-love and self-care. We all need our own space to nurture growth and have time for reflection. It may seem like a simple task, and for some of you, I'm sure it's already an integral part of your everyday routine. But for anyone who needs a little nudge, here you go: *It's super-important to etch out personal moments for self-reflection.*

Of course, it can be challenging if you have many external demands on you from work, family, and friends. They all come into play when planning out your day. And if you're like most people out there, including me, time for ourselves isn't always first on our list. Life is busy! Even if we recognize and value self-care as truly important, finding time for it is easier said than done. But it is definitely possible, and the benefits for your goals and feelings of joy are more than worth the effort.

Don't forget to take time for yourself. Set bold, beautiful boundaries, not only with others but in allowing yourself to have some ME moments. It's just as important for *you* to respect your boundaries too. This is self-love! Clear boundaries in all our relationships help us move towards living our *best life ever*.

Balancing in Personal Time

So many people need your time and attention that your own personal needs can sometimes get lost in the crowd of demands and commitments. Spreading yourself too thin prevents you from enjoying the delectable, thick layer of icing on the cake of life, which is (of course) living your *best life ever!* So, place some emphasis on self-love to add a cherry on top too. Pop in small pockets of time throughout your day for ME moments.

You're actually out of balance, if you're not taking time for self-care. So, here are a few tips to balance in some personal time:

Be direct with your intention when you need time off. If you clearly identify that time as being important to you, those who love you should respect your need for some brief rest and relaxation. Heck, most of us moms know not to refuse anyone a few minutes to sip on a cup of tea without interruption! That is a heavenly ME moment. Everyone deserves time to care for themselves, even if it's only for a few minutes. Carve out the time your inner-self craves!

Taking time to prioritize your needs will benefit everyone in your circle of life. Don't be pushed into something that doesn't feel right for you, if that gentle nudge is persuading you away from that particular direction. Stand strong in your values when pushed up against the wall by others. Creating healthy boundaries is one tool to benefit from increased levels of joy in your life. Creating healthy boundaries in your relationships will actually increase your connections with others. There will be less strife and conflict or confusion in your relationships, and you will feel respected and respect others in return. Determination is absolutely paramount in our personal developments.

Positive Affirmations

Create your own positive affirmations that leave you popping with positivity, or use these ones:

I am valuable. I have purpose.

I am worth it!

Feeling valuable begins with loving and believing in myself.

I deserve great things in my life.

I am strong. (i.e., Individually identifying your strengths.)

I am my own, personal cheerleader, cheering myself to victory.

I deserve time for self-care. Others need to respect my healthy boundaries.

I will accept compliments as the truth.

I am a confident, courageous, warrior spirit.

I am valuable.

I am lovable.

I am worthy of success in all areas of my life—harmonious balance.

I can turn insecurities into strengths by believing in myself.

It is truly important to encourage yourself not just in moments of self-doubt but each and every day. I know it's not always easy, but you are totally worth it. Honor yourself, for you are a valuable, beautiful warrior spirit.

Pop with positivity. Just like a kernel of corn, add the heat of positivity to make you pop! *Explode* with positivity, and destroy negative, self-sabotaging thoughts. Strengthen your connection with joy by having a positively pop-tastic day.

Stand stronger
rooted in your values

Chapter Fifteen
Value Your Values

"When values are clear, decisions are easy."
– Roy Disney

It is important to understand and honor your core values. Values are an essential tool to gain life balance, and for living your *best life ever*. It's a question of what is most important to you: faith, family, health, respect, or financial wealth? *Whatever* you value most is your core value in life. Your values need to match your actions. For example, if your strongest value is family, but you are not taking time to love and support them, then your values don't match up with your actions. Understanding our values creates awareness around what brings us the most joy in life and allows us to live life in more harmony. When our values and actions match up, an inner peace is present in all we do.

But wait! How does it really work? This is where we return to positive affirmations. Let's go back to 1911, which was a time when women used to wear huge, feathered hats. Psychologists back then noticed that those women always ducked while walking through doors, even when they were not wearing a hat. Things that you repeatedly do or say become your reality, and your body acts on them habitually. Saying positive things to yourself might sound strange to some of you right now, but if it helps you develop a continuous habit, your body will start working on those positive ideas. Like I mentioned before, the same thing works for negative affirmations. So, make sure your values are in accordance with your goals, and start encouraging yourself towards success.

Devaluing Your Worth

Do not speak defeat over your life. Psychology says that those who need to bully or knock others down do so out of their own insecurities. They may feel superior when they can assert their dominance over another person. It could also make them feel strong or powerful to beat another person. Next time someone is rude to you, rise above their negativity, knowing that it has nothing to do with you.

You have the right not to listen. Make up your mind to not let one person ruin your day. In your thoughts, distract yourself from sinking down to their negative level by secretly sending them positive vibes. Rise up with joy. Your cool composure will result in one or two things: They might rise up to your positivity on some level, or perhaps they become a bit miffed because you are not engaging in their negativity. Either way, you do not lose your joy.

If you find yourself being pulled sideways into negative self-talk, identify what's causing it. Most of the time, we are not aware of the negative patterns. Identifying and understanding the triggering, negative, self-defeating words starts us back on track to healing. Stop negative self-talk by reframing those messages as positive ones. I call this the reframe game—pass the negative over to a positive . . . to positively win at overcoming negativity! Give yourself the grace to make mistakes in this, as no one's keeping score.

Authenticity

A tree's strong hold is in the essence of its roots. Don't lose sight of your roots. Stand stronger rooted in your values. You need to stay grounded by connecting with the essence of who you are. Be authentically you—someone not afraid to show their true colors. For good or for bad, your true colors will always shine through, regardless of what you do to try and diminish their glow, so don't resist them. Focus on nurturing authentic growth in your life. Makes choices you can feel proud of. Be the best you can be, right where you are today, as each new life adventure starts within the present moment. Don't let pondering the past dull your day.

Embrace yourself by being true to you and not an imitation of someone else. The world needs you just as you are. They need your unique perspective, your unique look, and your unique abilities. Stick to what you know and be an expert at being you. It's what makes you so awesome. Be bold with the strength of joy, simply by believing in you.

I betcha your life is better than fiction. Your story needs not to be pretty or perfect, and it may not have happened the way you planned it, but it's *your* story and it's a part of who you are today. Your past doesn't have to define you; however, you can use your story to strengthen your spirit moving forward. Learning from our past experiences is a key tool to understanding how to improve and increase success. Let go of the regrets that hold you down, and free yourself of guilt. Be inspired by your own, authentic story.

Your true story might help someone else who is struggling with a similar challenge. You might not even realize that many people are facing similar challenges but are afraid to speak up about it. Use your story as a tool to propel yourself and others towards living the very *best life ever,* and set yourself up for an authentic future filled with genuine success.

Authenticity versus Perception

You don't need others to validate who you are. You just need to be true to you. Other people lack a 360-degree perceptive of the true you. So, don't spend a minute losing self-confidence over their inaccurate take on the authentic you. Take charge with a positive self-image. Define an image of yourself that includes all the amazing gifts and talents you possess. And, yes, juggling oranges or curling your toes is indeed a talent. Own all the amazing attributes that make you . . . you! You deserve to celebrate yourself. You deserve positive peeps in your life to encourage you towards your *best life ever*—even if that peep is you! When you see your reflection as you take that perfect selfie, make sure you're identifying with yourself as someone who deserves the very best in life. Never discount your worth!

Shine with self-love, and glow with pride. It takes so much courage to put your opinions first and be your own, personal cheerleader. When you understand this as your truth, and live your life with inner love, you will receive this same respect, love, and encouragement back from the world.

Don't give up your power to people who aren't cheering you on in life.

Resist the temptation to engage in their drama, and don't get tangled in their web of comparisons. Comparing yourself to others is always an uneven playing ground. Although neither of you ever have a chance of claiming a winner's trophy, both people involved are left feeling empty. Remember: Envy leaves you empty, so choose compliments, not comparisons. It is a great tool to inspire self-love.

A positive self-image is an important act of self-love. Most of us shine brighter when we follow the beat of our own drum. However, we can easily get distracted by another person's beat. It's tricky to avoid distraction when there's social-media perfection, self-proclaimed fabulousness, fancy photo filters, air-brushed everything, and catchy hashtags luring us in. We can be easily influenced by others, and it can sometimes feel as though it's sunnier in someone else's story. That is simply not true.

Please don't mistake when I'm saying here. I am a big fan of social media, and I love to scroll, but only when I'm doing it for the right reasons. Social media should only be used to enhance joy in your life—a fun way to connect with friends and family, or engage with your favorite celebrities or products.

Instruction manual not included.

It's become increasingly apparent in the last few years that you need to be skillful in maneuvering through social media to make sure it's a joyful experience. Understand how to compartmentalize what you're seeing and how your mind is processing those things. With millions of connections at your fingertips, social media has the potential to be an amazing outlet to experience joy when done right.

Let's look at the best ways to empower yourself to stay safe and keep your joy while connecting on social media. Censors and restrictions are great, but you, ultimately, need to be responsible for yourself and what you allow into your personal space and thoughts. When you do that, you will shine brighter and stronger as your authentic self.

Tips to Keeping Your Social-Media Experience Authentic:

Unplug. Limit your time—I've actually set a timer on Instagram. It's easy to lose track of time watching the cutest-ever animals doing silly stuff. Maximize the fun factor by setting *social-media* limits, and making sure to stay within it! Like all activities, balance is key to a healthy lifestyle.

Disengage with negative accounts. *Shhhh . . . they don't even need to know.* Muting someone's account is an easy way to discreetly disconnect. Connect with only accounts that inspire you, lift your energy or put a smile on your face.

Clarify communication. Let's face it, at times, texts can be cryptic. You send a message only to reread it seconds later to discover that you actually insinuated something completely different from what you had intended. Happens to the best of us. I'm the worst for rushing, and not rereading before hitting send—AKA, *the point of no return*—only to spend twice the time back pedaling with LOLs or apologetic excuses for why I sounded so discombobulated. Ahh . . . the modern joys of communicating via technology. Successful surfing or scrolling means staying true to you!!

Chapter Sixteen
Dust Settles. I Don't

"A wise girl knows her limits; a smart girl knows that she has none."
– Marilyn Monroe

Dust settles, but I don't. And don't you dare settle for anything less than the very best in life either. I implore you to rise above the dust and refuse to settle for a life of status quo. Best-life-ever status is what you deserve, so strive to thrive with a best-life-ever mindset.

You are not a dust bunny that gets caught behind the sofa and settles there for an extended period of time. You can't expect to grow and prosper in life when you're stuck hiding behind life's disappointments and hardships. The dust bunnies of the world stay stuck, lacking drive and eventually becoming dormant. Their only forward progression is the hands of time ticking by. Don't get stuck in the dust.

Dust bunnies look exactly like everyone else; however, they are isolated by their inability to recognize their full potential or worth, and they hold a depleted vision of their future. They repeatedly focus on their disappointments and failures, which inevitably becomes a personal pattern of identifying their shortcomings. Their shortcomings become their crutch to keep success out of reach, thus setting them worlds apart from the believers and the doers. Don't be fooled by their passive persuasion. Settling in right beside them will leave you feeling stuck too. Stay clear of the dust by focusing on achieving your goals and accomplishing your dreams. Never stop believing! You are the only one who can push your dreams forward, so take charge today.

Dust bunnies have little-to-no skill in self-motivation. A dust bunny's only chance of gaining forward movement in life is during spring cleaning—a cleaning generally initiated by other people's determination to succeed. Even then, those rascally rabbits might dodge the opportunity to be swept up in the momentum of other people's success. They dive further into the depths of a void-like existence, where lack feels plentiful and nothing seems to spark joy, at the same time isolating themselves from their passions and dreams.

Dust bunnies are challenged simply by maintaining the status quo, always feeling subject to circumstance. Dust bunnies are definitely not driving their dreams. They perceive everything as being done to or against them, perpetuating a feeling of lack of control over their lives. The dust bunnies of the world are always quick to point out the negative side to every situation. They never seem to see the cup as half full, or the sunshine behind the clouds.

A dust bunny resists change. They are not motivated to progress beyond their current circumstances, and they are settled in their dusty, non-driven ways. Everything to them is always fine, but never great, and they seem to have a short supply of joy in their life.

But most importantly, the dust bunnies of the world hold others back, and this could include you. They do this simply by projecting their negative slant on life, focusing on what has gone wrong, and taking little or no responsibility for the troubles that have come forth in their life. They will distract you from achieving anything more than a status-quo life. Misery loves company, and so do those darn dust bunnies.

Dust Yourself Off

I am simply stating the facts, and in no way slamming the dust bunnies of the world. They are good and lovable people. They've just become stuck in their troubles. Most of us know someone whose personality and drive fits this stereotype. They could be a loving family member or one of our dearest friends. I have several dust bunnies in my life whom I love deeply. I've just leaned over the years not to settle down into the dust with them. And they sure do love stirring up a dust storm!

Leave the dust bunnies in the dust, for I share in a bigger dream for you. So, dust off, and start working towards your full potential. You're worth it!

If this description of dust bunnies seems a little like a self-evaluation, no worries! Self-discovery is what this book is all about. Give yourself a hug, and then read on for more encouragement to hop off the dusty trail and gracefully move to a dust-free life. You've got this!

I hope you are already living a dust-free life, and that this chapter acts as encouragement and motivation to continue on your life ventures, recognizing that you deserve the very best. Or, perhaps, there are select areas of your life where you could use a little dusting off.

Stir up the settling dust in your life, and bring to light a best-life-ever frame of mind. Self-discovery begins with you. Explore your heart to understand whether you are living a dust-bunny kinda life. My prayer is that the dust bunnies in our lives will take witness of our upward momentum and see us achieving our best-life-ever status. I hope that will spark a flame inside them to aspire for more in life as well. We all deserve nothing less.

Status Quo, Yo!

Sure, status quo—keeping everything the same—seems like a cozy and easy option. But "cozy" isn't going to catapult you to achieving your dreams, and "easy" isn't going to help you get ahead in life either.

It is very easy to become complacent in life when everything is falling into place reasonably well. You're hitting status quo levels in all areas, and life seems easy-breezy, but you sense something is missing. Possibly it's that your passions are not moving you forward, making it difficult for you to connect with and experience true joy. There is an undefined lack in your life. You can't quite place your finger on it, but your heart feels an absence. What's missing?

It's simple. Easy-breezy isn't fulling your dreams and desires in life. Passions aren't popping. The lack of achievement in your life is disconnecting you from living with luster. "Status quo" is distancing you from a life filled with an abundance of joy—the joy you *deserve* in life. A quasi-comfortable life of status-quo is standing in the way of your *best life ever*.

Unquestionably, comfy feels good. Comfort is like a safety blanket in life. Yet it's in the uncomfortable times that we grow the most. It is when we are faced with adversity and in our most uncomfortable circumstances that we develop the strengths that define our destiny. It is in these moments that we begin to truly understand our full life's potential. Of course, it's not necessary to wait around for adversity to recognize your full growth potential. Pursuing your passions and goals will expedite growth. Step out of your comfort zone and stretch yourself to thrive in life.

Shifting out of your comfort zone will move you forward in life. You must be your own advocate. You cannot propel forward in life by always playing it safe. Launching forward will take some risk. I know taking risks sounds risky, but you're worth it. Adding a little calculated risk in life is no riskier than not taking advantage of all life has to offer. And it's not as mundane as continuing to roll along in the dusty trail of other people's successes.

As a child, self-motivation really wasn't my thing unless it involved watching endless hours of television or playing outside until dark, when my mom would hang her head out the back door and yell my name, usually whistling between each call, trying to grab my (and the cat's) attention! My parents tried their best, yet ended up enabling me more than anything. I was an adorable kid, and they never thought to push me. It wasn't until I was an adult and Jeffery encouraged me to go to university that I took a risk on myself and my motivation to learn. That risk paid off big time. Getting my bachelor's degree became something I am incredibly proud of.

Be a risk calculator by calculating each step towards success. A risk calculator inputs all the facts. Understanding every variable will help eliminate feelings of uncertainty. So, weigh out the pros and the cons, and ask, "Is it worth the risk?" Leap forward with faith, and remember that you first must believe it in your heart to see it happen in your life. Don't allow fear to paralyze your progress. Fear will stop success, so counter fear-based beliefs with faith. Use those fears to your advantage, for fear is a great deterrent from acting in haste. Explore your feelings of hesitation to validate whether this venture is the best move for you. Then head in the direction of success, trusting your intuitive voice. Our inner voice always seems to know what's best for us. Listen in and learn.

Never stop trying. Not every venture is successful. Assess what you've learned in the process. Dust off and try again. And keep on trying until you discover success. Push beyond your current routine to spark success in your life. Reminder, you've most definitely got this! You're most definitely worth it! Shine bright, for you are a star, not a depleted dust bunny.

Determination, Hard Work, and Grit

I imagine if you asked ten of most successful people what their greatest influencers of success were, they would likely say determination, hard work, and grit. I imagine that settling or keeping life comfy didn't set their success in motion. Their successes took commitment and stamina to achieve and maximize growth to where they are in life today. As I skimmed through countless articles that outlined the common traits of successful people, *determination, hard work, and grit* clearly topped the list of the most shared values among the most successful people in the world.

You deserve a top spot on the most-successful-people list too. Successful people are no more special than you and me. They've just worked hard, dedicated the time, and remained committed to achieving their goals, and you most definitely can too. So, stir up the dust, engage your determination, hard work, and grit, and start working towards your goals today. Each step forward is a step closer towards your dreams.

You are meant to succeed. So, don't get stuck in the dust or get caught being manipulated by others who will sweep you along, wanting you to work harder for them as they actively achieve their own successes, or sweeping you further away from your personal dreams and goals. Take charge of your life, don't let go of your dreams, and establish your own momentum towards success. Yes, life can become overwhelming at times, making it easy to become complacent or get stuck in adversity. Nevertheless, you are no dust bunny, so don't settle like one. Drive forward each day, focused on your dreams.

Achieve best-life-ever status by staying in the present moment. Take heed of what you desire most in life. Focus on pursuing these passions. Our *best life ever* manifests from our continual belief that we deserve better, and from focusing on achieving our personal goals. This pursuit will bring you lasting joy along the journey.

Instead of questioning "why," ask yourself "why not." Why not me? Why shouldn't I live out my dreams and live with an abundance of joy? Make bold affirmations that you are deserving of a magnitude of success and joy. Declare your dreams, and don't settle for anything less.

Maximize joy by maximizing your potential for success. If you fall, get back up and try again as many times as it takes to achieve your goals. Our spirit must be engaged in something greater than simply the status quo to thrive in a joyous life. Dwelling in displacement will eventually swept you further away from your dreams. Only determination, hard work, and grit will take you to the places you dream.

The Choice to Stay Stuck

We all have times in life when we feel stuck. It's up to you how long you stay stuck. It's your choice whether or not to cover up the discouragement with a comfy blanket of status quo, or step out of your comfort zone to maximize your time on earth. You only have one life to live, so I suggest you step out and step up. Realize that your cozy safety blanket was always, in fact, a miraculous superhero's cape of strength. You are super-capable of succeeding, so continue working hard. Keep going. Be your own superhero of success. Soar higher knowing you deserve a best-life-ever status. You possess the superpowers within your spirit to make your dreams come true.

When life feels like one endless struggle, and you start settling into a comfy, cozy, status-quo mindset, remind yourself that your current circumstances are only temporary. You have the inner strength to turn your situation around. Believe in yourself to connect with the powerful energy of joy. Be mindful of seeking joy, and in turn, joy will light your journey.

Don't settle into your limitations. Think limitless. Stay optimistic and seek other avenues to gain success in your life. Don't settle into the temporary job that makings you miserable, but stay determined! Use your current opportunity to learn, and let new goals propel you towards your dream position and career—yes, the one you deserve. Don't settle into the comfort zone, but explore new possibilities to create new opportunities. Don't settle for relationships that lack luster. Lift yourself with *self*-love, and discover the love and friendships you truly deserve. Don't settle in with peeps who aren't celebrating you, but surround yourself with people who lift the luster factor in your life to new heights.

Don't get stuck in status quo, as you most certainly deserve more from life. Do reignite your spark through self-discovery. Rediscover your passions, then reach out into this beautiful world to capture what brings you the most joy in life.

Chapter Seventeen
An Attitude of Gratitude

"There is a calmness to a life lived in gratitude, a quiet joy."
– Ralph H. Blum

When we take time to contemplate what we are thankful for in life, a feeling of gratitude comes up from our heart. Gratitude is simply reflecting on what we appreciate in life. It can be as simple as the roof over our head and the food on our plate. Or it can be as passionate as feeling thankful for the people who love us, for the opportunity to show them love, and feeling blessed with joyful moments on a beautiful journey. It is also giving thanks when everything in life isn't going perfect. Gratitude is when we recognize *all* experiences have value and meaning. Gratitude is one of the greatest gifts, giving us the grace to focus on what matters most.

Thoughts of gratitude enhance our focus on the many joys and pleasures available. Gratitude helps us cherish each moment as a precious gift. While an attitude of gratitude is more about being grateful *on purpose*, our attitude shapes our opinions, so if we can think about things that we are grateful for, we will believe that our life is blessed—a true gift. An attitude of gratitude is a way to increase the harmonious balance in your life. Proactively pursuing thoughts that inspire contentment, and feelings that promote positive emotions, creates a constant source of peaceful energy and positivity.

Gratitude is a simple yet very powerful tool to boost the energy of joy. Practice gratitude simply by pausing for a moment to ponder on what you feel most thankful for in life. Yes, it's truly that easy. You can aim your attention at absolutely anything that brings you comfort or joy. I've even launched a surge of gratitude sitting in traffic. The extra time in the car granted me the joyous opportunity to listen to a favorite song that randomly came on the radio as I was idling along.

I bet that you can think of countless opportunities that have set an attitude of gratitude in motion arising from an unexpected encounter. A spirit of gratitude turns unavoidable inconveniences into blessings, not burdens, while at the same time giving you joyful ME moments. And it helps you have a more harmonious flow forward for the remainder of the day. Simply being mindful of what you're grateful for can spark so much joy in your life. I guarantee an attitude of gratitude will generate genuine feeling of greatness within your mind, body, and soul.

Attitude Determines Altitude

One of my favorite quotes to encourage gratitude was coined by the late Zig Ziglar, a popular American motivational speaker, salesman, author, and philosopher. He said, "It's your attitude, not your aptitude, that will determine your altitude." Ziglar's quote emphasizes that your attitude determines your altitude, meaning our attitude plays a key role in determining how high we soar. Aptitude is our natural ability to do something, and shows itself in our gifts and talents. Ziglar is saying that you must possess a determined *attitude* to fully develop your aptitude. Your spirit soars higher with an attitude that's lifting, positive, and encouraging. Holding onto an attitude of gratitude goes hand-in-hand with this.

A distinguished and radiant eagle is equipped with a magnificent wingspan to majestically soar through the sky. An innate confidence empowers it to soar freely without limits. The eagle's limitless attitude inspires freedom. An attitude of gratitude will inspire a freeing feeling in your spirit to soar in the same way. By focusing on what you have, gratitude redirects your mind towards everything you are thankful for in life. Then you can view your life from new heights, letting the power of joy be the wind beneath your wings. Set your sights higher armed with a grateful heart.

A simple ME moment of gratitude allows us to direct our thoughts towards everything we feel appreciative for in life. When we engage in an attitude of gratitude, the joys in our life instinctually rise higher as well. A ME moment of gratitude gives us the grace to keep going, and grace releases an inner acceptance. When we reflect on what we are truly grateful for, we manifest an attitude of gratitude that warms our spirit.

Start today. Embark on redefining how you view your life. Adopting an attitude of gratitude will allow joy to radiate to new altitudes throughout your day.

A Victim Mindset Prevents Gratitude

From time to time, our thoughts fool us into believing we are a victim of circumstance. Fear paralyzes our thoughts and creates the illusion that we only deserve defeat and lack. Break down fear-based beliefs with an attitude of gratitude. Gratitude is a great practice to dodge the demons daring enough to distract you from achieving a best-life-ever status. The alternative is a role playing the victim, which is self-defeating. That creates a dismal existence of feeling sad, complaining about your lot in life, and criticizing others while taking zero accountability for your actions.

You don't want to be Academy Award worthy in playing the role of the victim in life. Your real life is not an elaborate plot against you.

Yet, identifying with this character will leave you disconnected from all the joys in life. A victim mindset creates a sinister sitcom that reruns in your narrative over and over again. You are not a victim, so reign victorious with a warrior spirit of gratitude.

Negativity and lack prevails in a victim-based mindset, leaving little room for feelings of gratitude. A person living within the constraints of a victim mentality centralize their attention towards everything that has gone wrong in the past, and they tend to predict that everything will go wrong in the future. They feel the world is against them, and they can never get a break in life. Their catastrophic thinking always points blame on other people and situations for their hardships in life. The victim is pessimistic and cynical. They feel threatened and powerless, like life hasn't been fair and has worn them down. When you encounter this, rise back up with an attitude of gratitude to strengthen your spirit.

Power up with an Attitude of Gratitude

Our thoughts hold the power to deliver us into a victorious glory, or to keep us static as a victim of defeat. I know life isn't always easy or fair—making it very easy to get trapped in a discouraging, defeated, negative mindset. Logic is telling us we deserve more; however, a constant stream of self-doubt and fear sets these notions aside. Streamline your thoughts back to victory by reframing them through the medium of gratitude.

Gratitude channels positive energy, just as a lake circulates currents of water to flow freely down a river to reach and replenish the oceans. Much like the river, gratitude is the vessel for positivity and joy to flow freely. A moment of gratitude releases many complex feelings that can rapidly generate the all-empowering happy hormones we discussed earlier in this book. Gratitude provides us with so much more than feeling thankful. It creates a sense of positivity, which encourages a peaceful and serene state within our spirit.

Immersing our thoughts in gratitude truly does direct our attitude towards joy.

Escape feelings of fear and doubt simply by exploring quiet moments of gratitude. Reflection is a powerful reframing exercise. Reflect on what brings you the most joy. Take charge of your thoughts by refocusing on what you are most grateful for in that very moment. Acknowledging gratitude is a gift of freedom that lies within us all. Focus on living a joy-filled life to free your mind from past fears and explore new possibilities.

The Chain Reaction of Gratitude

Gratitude sparks joy within us all. Joy promotes a feeling of gratitude in return. Recognizing what carries joy to your heart will most definitely spark a feeling of gratitude in your spirit. Any way you spin it, gratitude and joy lead you to victory. It's a win-win!

Sparking an attitude of gratitude initiates a chain reaction in your thoughts, and before you know it, the fireworks of gratitude are exploding and lighting up your spirit. Recognizing our true blessings in life develops our attitude of gratitude within our heart. This attitude can lift you through even the most challenging situations. The key to success is not to overthink it—it's not a skill-testing question! The skill is in understanding how to raise our spirits by connecting our thoughts to our blessings. Simply start by being grateful for all the small stuff that boosts your joy factor.

Here's how gratitude can initiate a chain reaction of joy in our thoughts: I am gratefully listening to the birds singing outside my window. My heart is humbled by the opportunity to feed the wild birds. My thoughts spiral to rejoice in the delight of nature. Onward thoughts center my spirit to bask in the glory of the sunlight that shines in the window as I watch the birds. I feel a love for life as I reflect on my fabulous family—an incredible husband who strongly lifts my wings so I can soar even higher with his encouragement and unconditional love, and my three amazing kids who astonish my soul, sparking a deeper attitude of gratitude within me. I could keep my spark of gratitude going forever. A magical momentum builds from a mind empowered by an attitude of gratitude.

This gratitude effect is explained by a study from The Mindfulness Awareness Research Center at the University of California, Los Angeles. It found that having an attitude of gratitude can change the molecular structure of your brain, keeping gray matter functioning properly, and it can make us healthier and happier. When you feel content and happy, the central nervous system is affected. You feel more peaceful, you are less reactive, and you are less resistant. These are such amazing insights to inspire us to be grateful.

How Gratitude Shapes Our Mental Health

The University of California conducted another study in which researchers recruited people with mental-health issues, including those suffering from depression and anxiety. The study had three-hundred adult participants who were randomly divided into three groups. All groups received counseling services. The first group was instructed to write one letter of gratitude to another person each week for three consecutive weeks. The second group was asked to write out their deepest feelings and thoughts about negative experiences, while the third group did not write anything.

Compared to those who wrote about negative feelings or those who merely received counseling, the group who wrote letters of gratitude reported feeling better, and they reported an improvement with their mental health twelve weeks after the experiment. This proves that shifting to an attitude of gratitude can reduce symptoms of depression and anxiety, while gratitude seems to establish a longer-lasting power to lift your spirits.

Here are a couple of other compelling studies on the benefits of adopting a grateful spirit:

Robert A. Emmons, Ph.D. from the University of California, Davis, and his colleague Mike McCullough at the University of Miami conducted a study on gratitude. They randomly assigned participants one of three tasks, and each week, participants kept a short journal. One group described five things they were grateful for that had happened to them in the past week. Another group recorded the daily troubles from the previous week that made them sad and angry, and the neutral group was asked to list five events that deeply affected them, but they were not told whether to focus on the positive or negative circumstances.

Ten weeks later, the participants in the gratitude group felt better about their lives, and their mental health got better too. They reported being 25 percent happier than the troubled group. The gratitude group became more active too, as they exercised 1.5 hours more every day. That's a powerful argument for gratitude, indeed!

In a separate study on gratitude, researchers from the University of California, Berkeley, identified how gratitude works on our bodies and minds. The researchers used an MRI scanner to measure the activity in the brain while people from multiple groups completed a gratitude task. During the task, the participants were given money by someone. This person's only request was that they pay it forward if they feel grateful.

The researchers wanted to know the difference between actions that are motivated by gratitude and actions that are driven by other motivations such as guilt, obligation, and what other people think. This study is important, because you can't fake gratitude. You need to really feel it.

The study suggested what's behind the psychological benefits of gratitude. Its report said, "Gratitude eliminates toxic emotions such as anger, sadness, grief, and jealousy. Gratitude has lasting effects on our brain as it can help change our perspective."

Reconnect Your Attitude to Gratitude

If you do not feel grateful, you can practice trying to feel thankful by keeping a journal. This could also be good for your mental and physical health. Take ME moments throughout your day and reflect on what you are grateful for. It doesn't need to be a grand gesture, but just something that you feel thankful for in the moment.

Sometimes, I hit my favorite bakery in the morning, buy a decadent and delightful treat for myself, and celebrate with gratitude and joy throughout the day. I tell myself that I am an amazingly awesome, deserving, beautiful, loving, kind, generous person, and I am rewarding myself with a delectable dessert. I don't eat it right away, enjoying this feeling of bliss and self-love, my mindfulness usually lasting until mid-morning before enjoying my sweet-treat, filling my morning with a magical mantra of gratitude, self-love, and joy!

Deliver yourself a delightful indulgence. Maybe it's treating your-self to your favorite latte, no strings attached—meaning owning, living, and loving every minute of your delicious, gratuitous, self-loving moment. Allow zero guilt, and only gratitude for a magical experience to honor yourself with some love. Maybe it's as simple as taking a stroll through the park on your lunch break or taking time to read your favorite comic. The important part of the equation is empowering yourself with gratitude via magical moments powered by joy. Allow yourself to get excited and own the opportunity to do something fabulous for yourself. Spark joy with an attitude of gratitude to make every moment count.

Wake up and shake up gratitude with praise. Acknowledge and recognize the many blessings in your life. Take them not for granted. Self-love is an act of gratitude, so identify your unique strengths to feel grateful and proud. Share your thoughts of gratitude by telling someone in your life that you're grateful for them. They will strengthen from your energy too. Volunteering or assisting others is always an amazing way to inspire gratitude. Celebrate the day as the beautiful gift of a new opportunity.

Giving Is the Gift

Invest in others, and let generosity be your gift to give. Plant a seed in someone else's heart. Recognize someone's talent. Get people to rise up to your giving nature—simply by setting an example. See what happens when you believe in yourself—when your mind is open to all possibilities. A genuine connection to other people motivates me every day to continue to spread the word of joy.

Mentoring is a gift that sparks gratitude in our hearts. Jeffery and I have always dreamt of establishing a home for orphaned children abroad—yet we held the limiting belief that our limited resources couldn't make a difference. Granted, as *big, bold, dreamers*, we metaphorically wrote this dream in permanent marker on our dream *wish list,* so we can revisit it. We've always felt extremely blessed and grateful to help out where we can. Among our contributions, we volunteer delivering meals to families in-need, foster children via World Vision Canada, as well as arranging an annual toy donation extravaganza—a very meaningful fun family tradition that sparks much joy and gratitude for us all. We also distribute hundreds of toys to local-area women's and children's shelters—I have precious pictures of a young Savannah and Sienna, and very little Liam, loading our vehicle with toys. After they were all snuggly seated, I'd proceed to pile *even more* toys on their laps and all around them—prompting a giggle-fest as I called out their names individually, pretending I had lost them *amidst the sea* of toys—a magical moment of joy.

Shortly after the COVID-19 pandemic hit, I began mentoring a young enthusiastic man with a big vision to help care for the homeless children in his community of Naibowa Parish, Uganda. Orphaned himself as a child, this young man understood the struggles impoverished young children faced. After several months of coaching/mentoring, he surprised Jeffery and I with the *honor* of naming his organization Joyful Children's Home, asking us to be co-founders as a thank you for our support. Since then, we've assisted him to legitimize his orphanage with government certifications while donating what we can to move the project forward. A shift in our thinking empowered the future.

Giving truly is the gift that keeps on going. And our limiting belief was debunked in the process—proving that even small steps towards your dreams can make a big difference. It was an amazing endeavor that Jeffery and I feel tremendous gratitude and pride to be a part of. A portion of the profits from this book will be given to help support Joyful Children's Home. I'm beaming at you with an attitude of gratitude for being a part of this process—the ripple effect of joy in motion!

Bloom and grow right where you are. Connect with a friend or loved one that you haven't reached out to for a while. Let them know you're thinking of them. Show them how much you care by taking a few minutes to call or simply send a text. Confess your love and admiration to your partner, kids, friends, or loved ones. Call your parents simply to tell them how much they mean to you. Share a joyful memory that meant a lot to you as a child.

Give a "Thank you for your welcoming smile" smile in return to the person you see each week at the check-out counter in the grocery store. Offer an, "Enjoy the beautiful day" to the person who held the door open for you when your hands were full.

Social media is an awesome platform to spread your attitude of gratitude. Facebook, Instagram, and tweeting your thoughts are only a fraction of the many ways to connect with others. All these are simple acts to empower an attitude of gratitude in your life, while at the same time increasing levels of joy. And these acts will most definitely bring joy not only to the recipient but will brighten your day too.

Grieve from a Place of Gratitude

There are many beautiful spirits I long to see again. Death is a part of life. When we've gone full circle, in the passing of a moment, it will be our time to move on to the next life. It's not important whether we accept this natural occurrence or if we live with in fear of its constant looming over our time here on earth. Either way, death is inevitably going to happen at some time or another. It seals our last stage of life.

For me, fearing death is a fiction made up by horror films filled with zombies, and ghosts hauntingly floating by—as a child I would sit alone watching this type of movies intensely—I guess you could say the thrill emitted much joy in my young spirit. I respect that all things continually change, and I look at death as one of those changes. I believe our physical bodies transform with our spiritual connection, and all those we've loved who've past on before us are eagerly waiting with open arms for our arrival in heaven.

So as this grateful joy seeker reflects on the loss of her father's precious presence while writing her book of joy, I encourage you to embrace even the heart-breaks of your life with gratitude and joy—balance out feelings of condemnation and sadness. RIP beautiful father of mine—I was blessed with your unconditional love and cheerleading in life.

Below, I share the poem I wrote on my twenty-second wedding anniversary, July 23, 2020, the day after my dad passed away, much too soon. I tried to capture tender emotions—a accurate, truthful impression of how grieving with gratitude felt for me. Grieving with gratitude doesn't undermine any of our emotions. Honor everything you feel, the joys as readily as the sorrows. It's only fair. "Unforgettable" articulated my immediate thoughts, releasing my most raw and authentic emotions and letting them emerge, and not simply anger and sorrow. Feelings of joy and gratitude surfaced as well.

Unforgettable

Tears overflowing my eyes,
Disbelief lingers in my mind,
As joy comforts my humble heart.
I admire and will emulate the light of your unconditional love;
A magnitude of gratitude glows as God embraces your spirit.
Freedom, peace, and eternal love embodies your being.
One last kiss to your forehead—
One last "I love you."
Your gifts an abundance of joyful memories, illuminated by love
shining brightly forever.

Grieving is tricky, and there are a lot of emotions involved. The process is very individual. We have a strong emotional reaction to the people we love, and when we have lost those people, it's extremely challenging to keep our joy.

I believe an army of angels is always looking out for me. So many loved ones who passed on before me now encourage me through many mediums. I have tremendous gratitude for these connections. In your process of grieving, remember the joyful moments. Remember why it hurts so much to have lost them, and remember the meaning behind the sorrow. In time, you will be able to extinguish some of the hurt that feels like a flame of sorrow in your heart.

Chapter Eighteen
Harmony

"Happiness is when what you think, what you say, and what you do are in harmony."
– Mahatma Gandhi

Set harmony in motion, simply by self-proclaiming a song as your very own, inspiring feelings of joy as you listen. My family selects a *song for each season*, or more truthfully, the *song is selected for us*, materializing organically in a meaningful way. Enchanting lyrics flow harmoniously, a soothing sound cheering us on throughout all life's adventures!

In 2014, we enjoyed the extraordinary good fortune of consecutive trips to Disney World and Disneyland. To all our delight, each time we hopped into the car for the trip, the hit song "Happy," by the amazing American musician Pharrell Williams, popped on the radio—a song that will harmoniously go down in the Cunningham history books as our family's anthem of that era. Just thinking of the song "Happy" prompts a joyful moment—a joy that fills my thoughts with gratitude. Such amazing memories of an abundantly *happy* time in our lives.

When I reflect on harmony, I think of music, a beautiful melody that lifts our spirits and warms our hearts. We all have our favorite songs that lift us up and excites our inner joy. While listening, our favorite songs prompt a sense of peacefulness that awakens the joy within us. Harmony is happening!

Music is an act of joy. Music is a powerful tool to inspire joy within us, whether it be classical, country, rap, rock, or anything in between. The harmony of a beautiful song stirs up our inner joy to dance with delight. A beautiful song can be euphoric, a virtual paradise within our mind, engaging our senses to soar, all of which stimulates the power of joy. Music is an amazing vessel to promote joy in your life. A feeling of harmony can result from the synergy that music and joy cultivate in our spirit. The perfect song can lift us when we're feeling low, or cause us to celebrate life within that very moment. Music lifts us while we listen and brings to light a joyful moment.

The beauty of a song tells a story to our soul. And stories connect us with the world. Music can most definitely bring us together in peace, joy, and love. Harmony is an endeavor to fuse peace, joy, and love as one within our hearts. Harmony filters through our spirit via the inspiration of music. A well-composed love song can enchant even the toughest of critics, and lead others to sing a joyful tune of love simply by spreading kindness, showing compassion, and loving inclusively. A passionate love song can top the eternal charts of unity. Set alight a harmonious glow by singing out to everyone you meet—leading with love.

The very first record I owned as a child was a *Sesame Street* compilation album, which included "Sing" by The Carpenters. That was truly my first favorite song. I would dance around the room singing strong, playing this beautiful song over and over again on my little red record player. The lyrics talk about singing a simple song of love for your whole life. It's a sweet song that still fills my heart with joy. It gives me a joyful moment every time I hear it, creating a harmony of love within my heart that can last a lifetime.

Harmony Is About Love

Harmony is about leading with love, and adding love to everything you do, by first loving yourself. Self-love will illuminate a shimmering light out into the world—a light that anyone around you can draw on to recharge their own inner glow with each act of love. Greet each new encounter with a glow that can only come from a heart filled with love. Flow forward in life with a freeing energy and reboot with love as needed. Love creates commonalities that can strike a chord of harmony within everyone's heart.

Lead with love and let go of judgement. When we lead with love, harmony happens for us all. When we are giving in love, love comes back to us in abundance. The energy derived by love is open and inclusive. Your glow needs no interpretation and has no space in your heart for judgement. Simply love.

When engaged, the energy of love creates a harmonious glow for us all to shine brightly together as in a sky filled with stars. Love is a powerful energy that boosts harmony, for love not only has the power to lift ourselves but is a powerful tool to boost others as well. Stand strong in the harmonious light of love.

Love has the capability to break down differences and strengthen relationships in a heightened, harmonious way. Love has the power to discover what binds us in solidarity.

Harmony in a Fragile World

The fire of a hateful heart, extinguished

by a river of love.

I wrote this quote after the murder of George Floyd, a beautiful man who made headlines when he was senselessly murdered at the hands of the very people society had put in place to protect him and

215

others. Police apprehended Floyd in a brutal and racially-motivated assault. While holding Floyd down, a police officer asphyxiated him by neck and back compression. As I write, that police officer is charged with Floyd's murder. My heart aches for Floyd's family and those others who suffered the same senseless loss of a precious life. We must continue to seek justice, muting the intolerable voices of hate.

I am a lifter, a leader of love, and a seeker of joy. I've made mankind my business, and I believe it should be everyone's top priority. Aren't we all human, first, before any other category like color of skin? Why prioritize anything else? Perhaps you are asking how can I talk of harmony at all when disharmonious acts like what happened to George Floyd plague our planet. I most humbly reply that all I truly know is that *change needs a starting point*. I will absolutely start stretching my open arms out to give the world a much needed, harmonious hug. I hope my encouragement of joy will began to help mend a most-fragile world.

Shine Stronger Together

Let a harmonious glow light each encounter with love,
and witness the energy of joy rise as strong as the sun.

We must genuinely pursue inclusive unity. We need a vision to globalize mutual admiration among all nations. Recognizing divisions between nations, and more specifically, divisions between races, demands a solution beyond balancing equality. Our individual strengths are like a beam of light—our collective rays shine stronger together. We become much more powerful when fused together by love, acceptance, and a profound respect for one another. We become as powerful as the radiant heat of the sun. Let love lead us to mutual admiration, with each of our unique gifts honored collectively.

When we recognize each other's individual talents as a gift for us all, we can truly embrace everyone's contributions equally.

It's my belief that harmony in a fragile world is an essential and achievable foundation for us to strive towards, so we can honor individual differences and eradicate racism and wars between nations. Our current alternative might prove fatal.

My greatest hope is that you will ignite the power of the tips and tools throughout this guide to increase the power of joy in your life. Increase your feelings of joy, release the energy of joy brightly out into the world, and create an awesome energy for others to mirror the power of joy within their own spirit. Let's interlink our hearts as one to inspire harmony in a fragile world, one loving encounter at a time.

Unity in Diversity

A fragile world can be mended with love. To mend a divided world—and particularly racial divisions—one person at a time is my sincere intent. The concept of harmony in a fragile world embraces all races, cultures, religions, sexes, genders, sexual orientations, disabilities, and ages. We need both empathy and determination to decrease inequalities in the world and *embrace our differences as our unified strength*—an undeniable strength that can unite everyone equally. That's how harmony will mend a fragile world. I realize it's not an easy feat; however, I unequivocally believe we all deserve to be treated equally.

The dictionary describes *unity in diversity* as, "An expression of harmony and unity between dissimilar individuals or groups. It is a concept of unity without uniformity and diversity without fragmentation that shifts focus from unity based on a mere tolerance of physical, cultural, linguistic, social, religious, political, ideological and/or psychological differences towards a more complex unity based on an understanding that our differences enrich human interactions."

I agree, and I believe our differences add the greatest gift to the world.

In this way, the concept of unity in diversity places emphasis on our differences being our light and our strength. Unity in diversity explores the idea that our differences hold the power to achieve unified strength. It's the idea that our differences are our best collective asset, displacing the belief that mere physical differences should drive division between us. More accurately, it's about defining our differences as the key connection to our complete wholeness. Our differences give us a collective wholeness, solidarity, and strength in the world.

Growing with Our Unique Gifts

Our differences offer the world a unique opportunity for growth to flourish in all areas. When we come together, embracing individual differences as our collective strength, we become each other's greatest ally. Unity sparks equality, equality sparks a greater feeling of joy and a greater sense of peace within the world.

The concept of *unity in diversity* encourages a harmonious equality that can empower us to mend the destructive notion that division is derived by our differences. Division is more largely the result of limited viewpoints and the inexcusable lack of love and respect for others. *Unity in diversity* highlights the value of our differences, recognizing that our differences are our most prized possessions. They are inner gifts brought forward by each of us to create a harmonious balance within the world. Being open to each other's inner gifts will welcome wholeness into our world.

Societal Change is Simple, but Not Easy

As I have frequently reminded you throughout this guide, simple doesn't always equate to easy. We must all be consciously aware of and actively seeking societal change. Small steps lead to big results. Everyone can make a difference. So, for the only time in this book, I will plead with you. I plead with you to lead with love, to create a harmonious world for us all. Let future generations only know of inequality of rights in the history books. Let them not bear first-hand witness to this horrific and shameful behavior. Let them see no more George Floyds in this world. Let's mend our fragile world with love, peace, and joy to strive for harmonious equality. We are *all* worth it!

Chapter Nineteen
Harmonious Balance

"Life blossoms when it is in a state of harmony and balance."
– Angie Karan Krezos

Living in harmony takes the idea of a balanced life to the next level. Harmony is the understanding that each aspect of your life is meaningful, and that only you have the power to add meaning to your own life. Harmony happens when you can live a balanced life that simultaneously drives your passions forward. Live a harmonious, balanced life by acknowledging that each situation can be seen in a joyful light. It's always a viable choice to seek joy, and it takes no more energy than feeling hopeless and discouraged. Spring into action with a joyful spirit to ignite a harmonious nature throughout each day.

It is said that harmony can bring a peaceful and stable order to society. And indeed, the definition of *harmonious* is that people or things go well together. When you get along with someone and rarely fight, you have a harmonious relationship.

Create a harmonious life by showing gratitude, being kind, honoring your values, and respecting others. And since all of these attributes encourage the energy of joy to flourish in our hearts, harmony and joy create a win/win situation! We should strive to make the world a place where harmony is synonymous with joy. We all deserve nothing less, for if we live from a place of harmony, we amplify joy within all our lives. While establishing joy, we (in turn) foster harmony. That's a beautiful vision to explore for us all.

Find a Place of Balance

It's truly important to cultivate harmony in our lives. Harmony is like bejeweling a balanced life. Harmony adds glitter and glow to living in balance. Find a place of balance by spending time nurturing each part of your life. Living in harmonious balance centers your equilibrium to emerge victorious within our mind, body, and soul.

Harmonious balance calms and takes claim over chaos. Serenity swivels our stresses right out the door. Peacefulness pivots us from the panic. Joy jumps over jealousy, and gratitude gleams beyond guilt to glitter and grow. Disastrous dealings of deceit can be dodged with determination!

Harmony and joy inspire a luxurious, illustrious life bursting with possibility. Open your heart and mind to accept these good things, and love will add luster to your life.

The Rhythm of Harmony

When I contemplate harmonious balance in my life, I think of a children's teeter-totter, like you might see on a playground. As a child, I always loved playing on the teeter-totter. It brought me so much joy.

My childhood home backed onto a beautiful, open space with a small playground, which included a well-loved teeter-totter. I fondly remember that it was electric blue with red and yellow seats. I felt lucky that I could simply hop over the fence at the end of our back yard and enjoy this area any time. The teeter-totter was definitely a favorite of mine. Although I ventured over the fence almost every day to play, my time on the teeter-totter was special.

As everyone who's enjoyed time on a teeter-totter knows, it works in partnership with someone else on the other end. Both participants must be engaged equally to maximize the fun factor. The natural rhythm of a teeter-totter evokes a feeling of harmonious balance between the participants, similar to our partnerships with others in life.

Back then, my family lived on a very quiet lane, and most of the neighbors were retired. Although I did enjoy some beautiful friendships and learned a lot from these wise, generous people, most of them were not the teetering, tottering type of friends. So, I was thrilled whenever a friend came to visit. I would almost always suggest going to the park to enjoy the chance to play on the teeter totter. It's a beautiful and joyful memory indeed.

The teeter-totter of life also involves partnership and balance, while stimulating joy in the moment. I believe balance brings happiness and leads us to enlightenment, while harmony brings us joy and serenity. Together, they create a serene feeling of peacefulness in knowing you walk through life strengthened by the power of joy.

Harmony in Each Interaction

You can bring harmony to each interaction, even when others aren't sharing the same harmonious vibe. When you rest in a place of inner peace, others can't engage you into their discontent. Each interpersonal interaction in life has potential for harmony. While harmony isn't always everyone's goal, we learn to maneuver through those relationships without allowing them to influence our thoughts.

For example, one afternoon, on one of the rare occasions when my older, adopted brother would give me the time of day, he agreed to play on the teeter-totter with me. Yet, soon after we started, he jumped off his end of the teeter-totter and laughed smugly as I plummeted to the ground.

Instantly, my feelings of harmony surrendered as I switched to survival mode! I had been abruptly abandoned to potentially capsize off the end of the teeter-tooter, while my brother had already run half the way home. But—plot twist—I didn't, in fact, capsize. I caught myself with my feet before hitting the ground. Hooray! I always love a happy, joyful ending!

Afterwards, I may have sarcastically asked my brother, with my parents in ear-shot, how his jump was. Other than that, though, I didn't make too much of a stink. It would only have satisfied his ego to get a negatively-charged rise from me, eagerly egging him on for future pranks.

The Value of Silence

Even way back then, as a young child when I didn't do much philosophizing, I still innately understood the principle that silence sometime speaks louder than words. I knew my brother would seek more enjoyment if I were to complain to my parents or get upset. Throughout the years, I learned that he found a lot of joy in tormenting me. He taught me valuable lessons about how a calm spirit rises with joy, and even though I didn't recognize it at the time, my silence acted as a means to stabilize harmony in my young life. I absolutely value that today. It is truly powerful. I find that I gain most of my insights and understanding of harmony from the disharmony shown towards me throughout my life.

The author and motivational speaker Steve Adubato, Ph.D. wrote that, "In the world of communication, silence often sends a powerful message. Not saying a word in certain situations speaks volumes, whether it is in a presentation, a negotiation, or in a heated debate or argument with a co-worker or family member."

LifeHack further supports the "silent response approach" by stating, "If we are silent, we send a powerful message that communicates that we don't agree or are not going along with what someone is saying."

Sometimes, harmony happens when we make a conscious decision to rise above disharmony with the blissful joy of silence. Harmony shouts out in silence.

Reroute Imbalance

Growing up, I tried my best to say as little as possible when dealing with my brother, while assuming his intent to create conflict was more mischievous than mean spirited. Regardless of the true intent, his actions still led to the immediate imbalance of harmony.

Reroute the imbalance others have placed in your path by having clear intentions for a resolution. Disclose your truest intent to lessen the disharmony. Be open and honest in your communication to lessen discord in the lives of everyone concerned. Life is a quick ride, so don't let other people steal your joy! Harmony has no room for jealousy or judgement. Instead, let the light of love lift harmony into motion. We all deserve to live in harmony, even if we must work hard to balance out the disharmony of others.

Reactions Are within Our Control

I shared the story of my brother and the teeter-totter to say that, even though we have no direct control over the actions of others, our reactions are entirely in our control. When we rise above someone's ill intent, which was meant to throw us off balance, we end up in victory and not as the victim. Thus, we release a harmonious balance to flow even more freely within our spirit. Let harmony lead you to a victorious life filled with love and joy, sometimes without ever saying a word.

Victory lies within us, and our most moving triumphs have little to do with conflict. Our greatest victories in life seem to surface after we break down our fears. External conflict doesn't have the same power when we learn how to move past or move forward with the fear. Our energy, whether it be positive or negative, shapes our experiences and returns into the world.

Dodging the disharmonious actions of other people has taught me a higher frequency of harmonious balance in my life. Learning to recognize the energy I *didn't* want in my life brought me closer to harmony. There's always a lesson to learn. Now, I have little tolerance for this type of discourse. And as I say with pride, I've learned to take the harmonious high road simply by disengaging from other people's strife.

Healthy, Balanced Relationships

Without cohesion within society the world experiences an unsteadiness; everything feels off-balanced. Without mutual respect, openness, and understanding, we can't begin to experience a balanced life. We must feel balanced with the rest of the world to preserve our harmonious glow. You deserve to glow without others dimming your light.

Establishing healthy boundaries in a relationship doesn't need to create conflict. Generally, you should discuss your feelings with the other person first. It's always wise to communicate your thoughts before cutting someone completely out of your life. But if they're the type of person who just doesn't listen or care, you might want to develop some boundaries. If they aren't treating you with respect anyway, you don't owe them an explanation, and you don't have to outwardly state that their negative energy is holding you back or causing negative emotions. Just back away from the relationship, be cordial and kind, and slowly distance yourself from that unhealthy relationship.

If you have someone in your life who is pulling you down, you need to evaluate whether they are a good fit for your life. Healthy boundaries provide you with a tool to develop positive self-esteem and to reconnect with what's important to you. Relationships aren't supposed to bring you down. Ask for help if necessary. You are not alone!

Identify fears that are holding you back from addressing these conflict-filled relationships, then work to release your limiting beliefs. Empower joy through positive affirmations and truly understand your feelings to promote harmony in your life. When we meditate a moment on the relationships in our lives, we can identify whether harmony is happening within those interactions.

Questions for Self-Discovery

Take a moment to ask yourself these self-discovery questions:

Do you feel like balance and joy resonate in your daily life? Do you love yourself unconditionally?

If not, identify what conditions you have placed on your love. Ask yourself what initiated these limiting beliefs. Then look at ways to lift these assumptions, as you most certainly deserve unconditional self-love. Healthy feelings of love begin by loving yourself.

Do you feel unconditional love from others?

If you do, list all the qualities they love about you, and then adopt them as the truth, if you haven't already. If you don't feel unconditional love from others, ask yourself if that is based on assumptions or actual fact-based conclusions? Is it your capacity to receive love or their ability to relinquish love? Let go of limiting beliefs or assumptions that could be holding you back from receiving the love you deserve. You deserve to feel loved!

Do you freely release love to nurture relationship with friends and family?

If not, then this is a great time to start. Send love out into the universe and receive an equal or greater amount of love in return.

Do you feel a sense of peace and serenity in your thoughts and interactions with society?

If you do, peacefulness will build a beautiful foundation for harmony. If not, what do you think is the cause of conflict? Are there tangible steps you can take to increase your feelings of harmony with others? How do you think that will change the way you explore the world? Perhaps your answer isn't a yes or no but rather a continuing journey of exploration. Maybe your thoughts led you to some place in the middle. Either way, honor yourself. And never forget that you deserve to live with a feeling of harmony in your heart. You deserve the peaceful flow that living in harmonious balance brings into your life. You deserve much love.

Love Leads to Harmony

Love leads us to a harmonious, balanced life. I pray that you find what brings you closer to rolling along with harmonious balance. To maintain a harmonious balance, we must adhere to our core values, follow intuitive nudges, and share a desire for peace and unconditional love, while respecting others with the same grace we give ourselves, and releasing bias against and judgment of those different to ourselves. We all deserve that respect.

When we discover balance within ourself and the world, the teeter-totter of life is placed in perpetual motion, evenly balanced back and forth by the cosmic energy on both ends. Maintaining balance feels good, like a resting place after a long journey. When we rise up with joy, the person on the other end feels your joy, and you feel theirs, too. You're both working towards the same goal. Harmonious balance is happening! A profound respect is balancing out each side. The teeter-totter of life perpetuates the love, faith, and happiness you deserve. Harmonious balance in motion is beautiful.

Harmonious balance creates a synergy between the powerful energy of joy and the stability of balance. It's an amazing, incredible combination that sparks so much positivity and gratitude over your life. Harmony is the product of the combined, euphoric, freeing energy of joy and balance. Stand strong in your commitment to strive towards harmony. An idea can only be placed into action if it is first made a priority in your life. Harmonious balance activates the energy of joy. Engage in harmony today!

Take Balance A Step Further

Are you enjoying what you do at work or are you just going through the motions? Are you happy within your home life, working towards a common goal to inspire harmony? Are you treating friends and family with love and respect, or are you working hard to create disharmony in your life by pushing them away, creating strife and being disengaged? Creating *awareness* around harmony is key to living your *best life ever*.

Answering these questions will help you develop your awareness. It's important to be an active listener. Are you always telling people what you know and never returning the favor by listening back? We have so much to learn from others. We learn and grow by listening, understanding, empathizing, and engaging with others.

Seek the Silver Lining

Aspire to living your *best life ever* by sparking harmony in your heart. Harmony brings to light a silver lining in each situation. It could be a momentous moment of self-discovery, a realization that something beautiful can arise even from the deepest shadows of despair, or simply that harmony is happening. It's often in your darkest hours of despair that enlightenment stirs up strength in our spirit, encouraging a ray of goodness to come out of life's deepest destruction.

The "silver lining" is a term that was coined in a poem by John Milton in 1634. Over the years, Milton's original words were translated into the more commonly known phrase we know today: Every cloud has a silver lining. Dictionary.com sums up these insightful words of wisdom best: "A sign of hope in an unfortunate or gloomy situation; a bright prospect," or, "A comforting or hopeful aspect of an otherwise desperate or unhappy situation."

The notion that every situation has a silver lining is a powerful tool to hold in your heart. It tells us there is magic in a moment of misery, for when our hearts are open to exploring all possibilities, even amidst the most catastrophic of circumstances, we can follow even the tiniest flicker of light away from absolute darkness.

We could say either of the following statements are truth:

1. There is much conflict, sorrow, heartache, doom, and gloom clouding over the world today.
2. There is much peace, hope, unity, joyful moments, and love as the sun shines on the world today.

Both statements are arguably true, yet the first statement suggests a grim, narrow, pessimistic view of the world, provoking fear and hopelessness, while the latter articulates faith and positivity for our world. Both take the same time and energy to express, but the results are completely different. Different energies in your life lead you in different directions. You are your only navigation tool, so follow the map in your heart.

Conclusion

*"You've always had the power, my dear; you just had
to learn it for yourself."*
– Glinda the Good Witch

Always remember: Joy begins and ends within your heart. Just as our
beloved Dorothy in *The Wizard of Oz* discovered, you too, my dear,
have always had the power to activate the all-powerful, lifting energy
of joy. Joy has been resting in your heart all along! You just needed
the opportunity to explore all the amazing possibilities it has to offer.
I believe that, deep down, you've always known this, and I base my
bold assumption purely on the fact that you picked up this book and
have now read it to the end.

This deliberate intent to thrive speaks volumes about your warrior
spirit and your commitment to living your best life. You have an
intention to thrive with joy, initiated by your very own intuition,
which was what first gave you that tiny, gentle nudge in the direction
of joy. It sounds serendipitous to me. So now, take your inner power
of joy and continue to intentionally seek joy along your journey. You
deserve best-life-ever status, and don't you dare forget it!

Yay! You've finished reading this guide! It's self-gratitude time!
Completing an important goal is always a joyous celebration, especially when you've gained valuable insight to further magnify your
intrinsic ability as a joy-seeker. Although, truth be told, the real

joy-ride has only just begun! I merely sprinkled a little pixie dust on your heart to blossom your seed of joy, as it grew deeper roots for success.

Now, it's your chance to set into motion the tips, tools, and enthusiasm from this guide to catapult yourself to new heights simply by tapping into the magical power of joy. My greatest intention and sincere hope for you is that, in the pages of this book, you've discovered a more intimate relationship with joy. And that you start today to engage the energy of joy, which will provide a constant stream of strength in your life.

On our journey of joy, we've explored happiness, faith, gratitude, harmony, peace, and love as key pathways to harnessing the energy of joy. We've also explored our warrior spirit, the empowerment in running our own race, the astounding advantages of a present-moment mindset, how to rise above the dust bunnies, and so many other amazing avenues to direct our thoughts to hold onto joy.

We also affirmed that you are the *magic* in the moment; you are a *shiny, bright, beautiful* person who deserves all the luster of life. Remind yourself that you've got that little something extra that makes you *extraordinary*. It's extra important you always remember this! You are a perfectly imperfect, fabulously flawed, awesome you! Life isn't perfect, and you can't hold yourself to unrealistic expectations, if the world can't either. Keep in mind that *perfectly imperfect* lends itself readily to the real world. Embrace the powerful energy of joy as a shield protecting your heart from external forces that try to keep you from living your *best life ever*.

Now you have the bold, brave courage you need to consciously apply all these warrior superpowers directly into your life. These are powers that activate your senses to thrive, while at the same time, providing you with a heightened awareness to easily tap into the powerful strength of joy, raising your spirits, whatever the circumstances.

I hope a peaceful revolution of joy has ignited within your spirit. I would love for you to soar to immeasurable heights in life simply by believing you deserve nothing less! Begin your own self-guided journey with joy. That is the real adventure that awaits you now.

You've got this! You're most certainly worth it. Now, go ahead. Seek joy for yourself! EnJOY life!

Truly wishing you a joy-filled ride, sincerely, your friend and fellow joy-seeker,

Kelley, Xo

ABOUT THE AUTHOR

With a Bachelors degree in Sociology and iPEC certification as a *Transformational* Life Coach, Kelley Cunningham is creator, owner, and CJO (Chief Joy Officer) of JoyINC., a solution-focused coaching company that partners with people to achieve their life goals, and beyond. She's been invited to speak as a "joy expert" across North America, and appreciative of numerous accolades along the way, which include an invite to write a piece for the book *Unzenable* and being featured in the online magazine *Positivity.*

Kelley is a Canadian who takes much pride in her Métis Indigenous and Scandinavian heritage. She lives in the Toronto area with husband and soulmate Jeffery. They have three beautiful children: Savannah, Sienna, and Liam. Additionally they enjoyed many charmed years living in the U.S.A. They cherish time together, traveling and learning about other cultures. Their family also includes Teddy Bear and Blu Bear, their sweet Chow Chows, and their beloved adopted Persian cat Princess Leia.

Kelley loves to run, yoga and vegetarianism—she is an avid conservationist, as well as a children's and animal rights advocate. She is a global mentor and co-founder of Joyful Children's Home: a orphanage in Naibowa Parish, Uganda. A portion of the proceeds from this book will joyfully go towards supporting many non-profit charities.

Printed in Canada